Common Nonsense?

A Practical Guide to Managing Through Emotional Intelligence

Leadership Through Emotional Intelligence Volume 1

Common *Nonsense?*

A Practical Guide to Managing Through Emotional Intelligence

Leadership Through Emotional Intelligence Volume 1

Susan Fink Childs, FACMPE

Lophiiform Press

ISBN-13: 978-1-953134-05-9 hardcover
ISBN-13: 978-1-953134-06-6 paperback
ISBN-13: 978-1-953134-07-3 ebook

A 25 & Y Original   25andY.com
First Edition: November 2020

Cover Design by Svitlana Stefaniuk
Interior Design by Sebastian Penraeth

Published in Denver, Colorado
Printed in the United States of America

10 9 8 7 6 5 4 3 2 1

Dedication

To Mom, who said, "You're the only one that has to live with yourself the rest of your life."

Table of Contents

Foreword

by Frank Cohen

If I was a teenager, I would probably write, "OMG. Susan really nailed this." Actually, excluding the OMG, I am happy to say that Susan did, in fact, really nail this topic. The topic of leadership is oft times treated as an eclectic concept, with many different definitions of not only what is leadership but what constitutes a good vs. a bad leader. In her book, Susan transcends the eclectic nature of this highly diversified and brings home a more dogmatic approach, assuring a more concise, united and wholistic approach to this idea of leadership. And how much timelier could this book be! Being an effective and positive leader is always important, but here and now, in the middle of a global pandemic that promises to challenge the role of leaders perhaps more than any other time in our history, it is perhaps the single most important aspect of our financial and business survival. At the time that I am writing this introduction, I have healthcare clients that are projecting losses in the hundreds of millions of dollars. Entire departments have been furloughed. Telehealth services have increased by orders of magnitude and, for all intents and purposes, it would appear that we are winging it in way too many areas. I believe that you can tell more about a person in five minutes during a crisis than you can at any other time. Being able to manage a crisis effectively is, in my opinion, the most important role of a leader.

One of my favorite movies is called *Heartbreak Ridge*, starring Clint Eastwood, and I believe he is the one who originally coined the phrase "improvise, adapt, and overcome," now a common expression amongst US Marines and special operators. In her book, Susan speaks to the importance of this idea specifically. Perhaps my favorite part of her book, however, are the stories and anecdotes. Both funny and appropriate at the same time, Susan uses brilliant prose to bring together complex ideas in a way that everyone can understand and apply the principles. Perhaps my favorite was the story, "Stay in the Lines? Or Outside with Wild Abandon?" So as not to be a spoiler, let me just say that I was so able to relate to the destructive nature of the "my way or the highway" approach to leadership exemplified in this story.

I am an avid student of the human brain and never cease to be fascinated by how amazing it is. Making up only 3 percent of our body weight, it consumes 25 percent of our calories on a daily basis! So, no wonder my favorite chapters were those on Emotional Intelligence. Without getting into the nitty-gritty details, Susan beautifully explains the link between high emotional intelligence and effective leadership, and I would venture to say that the latter simply cannot exist without the former.

One of my favorite quotes is from Bill Taylor, from his article entitled "Did you Pass the Leadership Test" and it goes like this:

The true mark of a leader is the willingness to stick with a bold course of action—an unconventional business strategy, a unique product-development roadmap, a controversial marketing campaign—even as the rest of the world wonders why you're not marching in step with the status quo. In other words, real leaders are happy to zig while others zag. They understand that in an era of hyper-competition and non-stop disruption, the only way to stand out from the crowd is to stand for something special.

In general, Susan has addressed every important component of leadership, leaving no stone unturned. And as I stated before, while this is important during normal times, it is absolutely critical during abnormal times and one would be hard-pressed to find a more abnormal time that what we are dealing with right now. So, kudos to Susan. If you are in a leadership position or would like to be sometime in the future, this is required reading.

Preface

"Do not go where the path may lead. Go instead where there is no path and leave a trail."

"The only person you are destined to become is the person you decide to be."

Ralph Waldo Emerson

The Conscious Decision to Lead and Support

The delivery of care today will shape the practices of tomorrow. As practice leaders, it is our charge to combine the finest features of traditional care and transform those best practices to a newly balanced focus on the pivotal relationships between the physician, patient and … us!

What is the drive and balance that keeps us motivated and personally committed to improving the quality of patient care? How do we imbed more traditional patient-centered processes with newer therapies and technological advances?

A superior leader is a person who brings people together—some playing that role without formal recognition—to achieve exceptional results. As with other conditions in our life, there are times when we may not have chosen or even preferred to take on that responsibility. We are instead thrown into a new management position or unexpected promotion. If you find yourself in that position, first remember: if you were not stellar, you would not have been elevated to a new level of professionalism. This book will help you make that transition a successful one, allowing your actions to reflect your leadership and capabilities. There are many people and resources to work with and expand your knowledge as you move your team forward with positive guidance and direction. This book will help you access those resources.

Together, we will research approaches to healthcare administration, comparisons of past and current dynamics, important trends, and care needs from all perspectives: administrator, patient, and physician.

Practices need to pay attention as patients' expectations continue to rise with each and every encounter. As we enter into new spheres of care, we must be more aware of patients' anticipations and how to gain and sustain their active engagement.

What kind of care is it that they really want? How and when did these essential factors change? We have to conserve and keep cherished foundational priorities front and center in patient care. The patient and physician are the center of the universe. Everything else around that is support.

My mother said that there *has* to be a conversation between the physician and the patient. My aunt says that a personal touch is always needed.

Patients are a bundle of emotions. The rest of us continue to complete the circle of care to strengthen the patient's experience from placing the appointment to getting the claim paid—the first time!

We will examine real-life cases from patients evaluating their priorities and unhappy occurrences and offer proven solutions and a plethora of examples.

Administrators are the central fulcrum of the entire practice. We choreograph and communicate visions, build bridges, and establish boundaries. A physician once said to me that managers are the barometers of the practice. This is so true! And it is why it is imperative for administrators and physicians be perceived as a unified team. This relationship can be built soundly by balancing mutual support with checks and balances. We administrate according to practice goals and missions, and physicians should be aware of personnel trends, operational successes, as well as operational challenges.

We will discuss how leadership can continue that accord by clearly conveying practice priorities that involve and engage every employee. Tried and true communication styles are associated with esperiences that are embedded in daily interactions, techniques that sustain gained trust and improve work performance.

This book offers a complilation of lived experiences, lessons learned, and pearls of wisdom that can help with everyday leadership for administrators and physicians, with some likely being introduced as new concepts while others can serve as a gentle reminder.

The more things change, the more they stay the same.

But patients are not data streams, and technology does not have a heart.

You will find thought-provoking and topical questions for peers following the final chapter. These queries are great conversation starters and points for discussion forums, including meetings, round tables, and workshops.

We honor the medical profession's most vital and fundamental concepts of care when we share our finest hard-earned features of time-honored and established care.

Let us look at our journey and how we can establish our individual footprint of care—partnered with the most beneficial technologies—towards a newly recalibrated relationship!

Introduction

When Your Daughter Buys You an
"Anti-Stress Kit" for the Holidays

Balancing Personal
Life and Work

A principal reason some do not aim for administration, executive, or C-suite management is because they do not want to sacrifice a work-life balance.

It's sad but true. Work-life balance is difficult, and sometimes, even when we think it's all under control, we are not aware of our own anxiety or stress levels. But those around us see it, and we should listen when they speak.

When my daughter was in the eighth grade (she was in the seventh grade when she asked why I volunteer for so many things) it became evident to her that I needed to relax. I remember one distinct moment one evening when my son commented on how much I work. Mind you, I did not really mind working that much. Not recognizing the imbalance was part of my problem.

Thus, my present for the following holiday was an anti-stress kit: a massive and beautiful bouquet of lovely scented bath items to make me feel like I was on a tropical island. I thanked her, becoming suddenly aware that I needed this more than I had realized.

For me, one of the biggest issues impacting my ability to manage my work-life balance is that I do not have a crystal ball to see what is needed for the next step of healthcare. As administrators, our job is never done, and there always seems to be numerous moving targets. It is extremely easy to experience a constant escalation of work-related activities that answer the need for information but cost us the life balance we also need. I have found a few avenues that allow me to remain as current as possible while leveraging the shared effort of other administrators pursuing the same goal. By gathering resources of internal and external indicators, such as list serves, face-to-face meetings, and other professional connections, I have been able to leverage others' resource gathering to amplify my own.

Another opportunity to proactively prepare for changes coming down the road is to keep in touch with payers as to their most recent offerings and upcoming changes. These relationships are beyond crucial as to their substantial impact on the growth, strength, and life of the practice. We are then able to have a controlled response for needed changes. Keeping the patient as first priority, offering compassionate care and aware of most recent events, can affect our practice in the most progressive ways.

Additionally, it helps to prioritize needed next steps to fend off surprises by listening to our patients and implementing the style of care they request, for example, longer hours, earlier appointments, or improved access. This helps administrators identify most current patient concerns and keep on top of what is yet to come. This can lead to a very positive path forward for the practice.

The following chapters will expound on these ideas as well as other important details that will allow you to grow your personal satisfaction with your job, your leadership skills, and the success of your practice.

On a personal note, please remember to have lunch! (And not in your office.)

I Love My Job!

One most important factor in a successful relationship is a positive attitude towards our role. We love coming to work when we feel a purpose and devotion to what we are doing. It fulfills one or many needs. An April 2019 CNBC survey asked 8,664 professionals which of the following categories contribute the greatest to a happy workplace:

- Meaning
- Autonomy
- Contribution
- Opportunity
- Pay

The survey found that it was providing opportunity for workers to advance their careers that may be the best way to keep them from leaving. Just thirteen percent of workers who say their companies provide "excellent" opportunities for advancement were thinking of quitting their jobs.[1]

Our job as managers is to do just that: help people relate to their work and see how it helps our patients.

Again, we are in the very best industry to see and feel the effect of our work. As patients heal and treatments are successful, and even when they're not, we are truly making a difference in someone's life. That is quite an impact for one's affirmation.

Some say that separating your work and personal life simply cannot be done and define the issue as work-life integration rather than calling it work-life balance. Again, I love my work, but there must be time for a break from our jobs to relax. It is essential to one's physical and mental health. No one ever retires and says they wish they had worked more! We can call it any term we choose. Inevitably, it is our choice, and a holistic experience can be achieved.

A Healthy Work Environment

Let's first look at a healthy work environment—one where pressures on employees are relevant to their abilities and resources, the amount of control they have over their work, and the support they receive.

The concept of stress at work is often confused with a challenge, but these concepts are not the same. Being challenged can motivate us psychologically and physically. We feel energized and satisfied. It can also motivate us to learn new skills and lead to mastery in our jobs.

Challenges are an essential ingredient to being healthy and productive at work. Even when it feels too much, as we feel support, and support others, it works!

To me, an excellent example of a challenge and good stress is just as you are falling asleep after working really hard, you reflect on having gotten so much done that day, and you feel really good. That is a *delicious* kind of tired.

Writing Can Be Releasing

Part of good stress is releasing when needed in a productive way. Sometimes when you just need to let it out and don't know what to say, writing something down is a perfect way to release the tension and allow you to express yourself freely and honestly. The key, of course, is to determine which version is the best to convey or if it needs to be said at all. It is all part of a process of how you may handle and express information.

Consider Abraham Lincoln, who as a young man learned a very valuable lesson about writing something inflammatory and making it public. In 1842, he publicly embarrassed a politician named James Shields in a local newspaper. This was not taken lightly, and Lincoln was challenged to duel which was only canceled at the last moment!

He continued to write a response if he greatly disagreed with someone—and then never sent them. Some of these letters were found after his death. When you think about it, this action served a similar purpose as a personal journal, where someone is able to express themselves privately, freely, and honestly when confronting a difficult situation. Which can allow them to let it go.

This is a great example of an emotional intelligence process where you can be conscious of your emotions and reactions, then controll and guide them in the most positive manner.

Consider this process when you are tempted to send an angry email: send it to yourself first, allowing a delay for it to be received such as 30 or 45 minutes. This may be enough time to allow you to cool off so that when you receive and re-read it, your perception may be a little different and you may choose not to send. This is similar to when your mother said to count to ten before you respond. If ever in doubt, give yourself an extra chance, because once you send—it's out there.

Another emotion enhancer is a gentle scent. Being mindful of other's sensitivities, your own private aromatherapy is in reach. It is not unusual for people to have oil diffusers in an area for a calming scent. And now, there is no longer a need to wait for the diffusers to begin working or to fill a large area. Aromatherapy offers small nasal inhalers you can use when needed for an instant calming experience. The vapor also opens airways with a burst of aromatherapy that wakes you up and helps your brain focus.

Niksen

There are also times when we all would like to do absolutely nothing!

There is a marvelous Dutch concept called *niksen* that allows yourself to be in an idle environment. Carolien Hamming, managing director at CSR Centrum, a coaching center in the Netherlands that helps clients manage stress and recover from burnout, offers this description of the practice: "You don't act with purpose, neither physically or mentally, and you let your thoughts all go freely." [2]

Niksen is not a trendy concept in the Netherlands, but part of their daily vocabulary. It is a sort of neutral state of mind that can very easily occur naturally, as when a person daydreams, but busy people who have set that childish practice aside can find it difficult to return to doing. Mindfully setting aside time for this sort of do-nothingness can improve problem solving and creativity, while also reducing stress. The more often it is practiced, the easier to repeat.

Think of a time where you were perhaps a passenger in a car or train and looking out the window. It is almost a calm dreaminess where you are semi-aware. A quiet non-committal peace. This can be done for minutes or longer. And has perhaps for too long in America been considered a negative trait.

Niksen can be a guilt-free approach that benefits every person on a healthy, open, and creative level.

When Is Your Peak Time?

Each of us has the time of day that we believe we tend to work to our maximum potential. Usually you are a morning person or a night person. If you are able to arrange your schedule around your personal best behavior, I strongly suggest doing so. Even without the luxury of dictating our own schedules most of us can still take advantage of timing our capacity for the most efficient and best professional behavior.

Following this natural flow, a good practice is to try to schedule our toughest meetings in the mornings if we feel that is usually our strongest time. No one knows your energy patterns better than you. We all know what is best for us. Tune into that emotional intelligence, fully aware of yourself and others. Planning in partnership with our most productive timing is certainly a positive approach that can work with each of our natural tendencies and preferences.

Get Help, Get Out, and Get Moving

And sometimes, we could use a little assistance. One example—who says it does not take a village? The Rwandan prescription for depression is sun, drum, dance and community. They noticed that depression therapy from Western visitors included sitting and discussing their problems in a dark room. The Rwandans could not see how this would bring anyone out of a depression.

Their treatment is to get one's blood flowing again with dancing and drumming in the sun. The intent is for the entire community to be able to come together and lift all present back to joy.

Not many of you will be able to summon precisely this sort of activity, but it would be good to think about ways to include this kind of community and energy in your life.

Getting the Right Kind of Sleep

We seem to be more aware when able to get that good quality sleep, which is also very good for the brain. According to the National Sleep Foundation, adults from the ages of 18 to 64 is likely to need anywhere from seven to nine hours of sleep[3] for their best performance. Any variance from that can actually impact your daily accomplishments and momentum.

One reason is that as we sleep the brain removes a toxic protein called beta-amyloid from its neurons. These by-product proteins of neural activity build up during your waking hours. This toxic protein is also known for accumulating in the brains of patients with Alzheimer's disease. Your brain can only sufficiently remove these toxic proteins when you have enough quality sleep. If not, the toxic proteins may remain in your brain.[4]

This build up can affect your ability to think and slow your problem-solving abilities and sufficiently process information. There can be increased anxiety and a reduction in creativity. Learning how to regularly achieve high-quality sleep pays for itself in a very short time. One approach is to begin your nightly routine an hour earlier, and hopefully you will be able to asleep earlier. Lifestyle dictates everything, including sleep. Build time in for this much-needed bodily function as you would any other priority. Coming as close to the daily requirement as you can is all anyone can do. Good night and sleep tight.

"If you choose to not find joy in the snow, you will have less joy, but still the same amount of snow."

Thich Nhat Hanh

Eat the Healthiest Food for Most Positive Behavior

The high-stress requirements of a job as an administrator and leader can easily result in burnout. And burnout, unfortunately, can lead to depression. It has been found that improved nutrition can actually address and help treat this sadness.

Researchers in Australia reviewed whether improving the diet of people with major depression would also help improve their mood. After twelve weeks, the people who improved their diet showed significantly more positive moods. Research suggests that a Mediterranean diet full of fruits, vegetables, seafood, olive oil, and lean meats can prevent and even treat depression. Some medical schools, including Columbia University's Vagelos College of Physicians and Surgeons, have taught psychiatry resident students about the vital impact of diet.[5]

On the flip side, a bad diet can also affect the micro-organisms that live in our digestive tract. These are the molecules that define the production of serotonin found in our brains, which directly impacts our functional capabilities. I am confident that we always want all of your capabilities to be (at least) 100 percent!

Gardening Grows and Heals

Dr. Oliver Sacks was an author and neurologist who saw gardening as an essential part of creativity because it is calming and invigorating at the same time. Whether in pots or acres of land, working with plants and soil can be very therapeutic. In fact, Dr. Sacks wrote, "In forty years of medical practice, I have found only two types of non-pharmaceutical 'therapy' to be vitally important ... music and gardens. I have seen the restorative and healing powers of nature and gardens. In many cases, more powerful than any medication."[6]

Need a Reprieve?

We are made up of more than our occupations. It is okay to put in the extra time—we all do. But, ask yourself: are you bringing work home *every* night? These not-so-healthy habits tend to grow.

Protect yourself as needed. Have a private safe space to reflect and regroup. It can be your office, a walking path, or any area where one can have some personal time. Part of burning out is not being able to recharge. Go and recharge!

How to Detach and *Really* Relax

There was a time before mobile phones when vacation and time away from the office was just that—you could truly get a break from work. It was much harder for people to get in touch with you. I am sure you have tried contacting someone and gotten the out of office response that includes they will be "unreachable with limited access to the internet." And to "please contact Melissa at ..." Yes, that message. You too can be one of those individuals. Make it happen. This is a more than appropriate time for it to be perfectly okay to delegate a few tasks while you are gone.

If you find that your need for control keeps asserting itself, fight that habit and leave that message! You can address any issues after you have had a break. Grant yourself the use of your hard-earned vacation days to experience some personal time. It feels really good to return to work refreshed, prepared, and energized to attack whatever you find on your desk!

If you find this concept challenging, I suggest beginning with small increments. A day here and there is a very nice pause. Even if you end up having only a very brief respite, that's more than you may have seriously considered before reading this. Please try it.

Even with all the steps and buffers, be aware of what your own body tells you. Stress reveals itself within you. Pay attention to signals that may occur so you may identify and act upon as soon as possible. An example? Think about the stomachache you may feel first thing in the morning because you are nervous, or aches and pains as they can accumulate as a result of stress and anxiety. Or what wakes you up at 3:33 every morning!?

Disconnect physically from work. Consider and protect your home as a safe place by removing yourself from devices that remind you that there's work to be done and could easily distract you back towards that work. Cover things. For example, hiding your laptop in a closet will keep work out of sight and out of mind.

If you are able, try a private ritual for before or when you arrive home, such as exercising, walking, gardening, or a cleansing shower. Even with children, we can find a way. I have a friend who would arrive home and within five minutes he and the kids would be jumping in the pool for instant quality family time. For some, it is music. Whatever your preferences, let them be ones that replenish you.

Even Better, *Schedule* a Vacation!

Even a few days in a row away from the consistent pressure and demands can be a great invigorator. Your family and others that can help you focus on enhancing our personal life can be a great support and strengthen your efforts to maintain a balanced life. Your body will go through a natural process when allowed this sort of respite, and you should be able to get a little more sleep, which will help your brain and relax your body.

Let your body care for itself, not depending on something else to do so. Although it might be tempting to try for a quick fix, please do not depend upon sleeping aids or other substances that can throw your entire body and mind off balance. This is where feeding your body with natural and nutritious foods will truly nourish with the best energy.

By now you see that most of your time is at a premium and never really your own. Administrators are "income generating space," which clearly declares the essential need to care for ourselves, so we are prepared and fully able to take care of everything (and everyone) else. Predict and protect your time and privacy wherever you can. Review your voicemail response timing as well as other communication avenues to allow and build in a realistic buffer period so you may better choreograph meetings, conversations, and reports into a more predictable workflow. Every little bit helps.

Our parents were correct. Even ten minutes outside is a break that we all can benefit from. Just moving physically also revives us a bit!

"If I am not good to myself, how can I expect anyone else to be good to me?"

Maya Angelou

To completely disengage from work, plan ahead! It does not seem to matter whether we are gone for three days or a week, the result is the same. We are only human and there is only so much we can do. We know the potential bottlenecks or issues that are most likely to occur and what *must* be done before we go.

Arrange for that and you will discover that the world can live without you, for a little while at least! That is okay. This can also clarify what a great team you have as well. Very affirming for all.

21

2

Returning to Why We Are Here and Listening for What is Next

What Can I Do Now?

While it can be challenging, developing a culture that places a premium on trust, honesty, and stellar communication is the goal that requires model support. Reward good behavior and place programs and procedures in place to stamp out destructive and dysfunctional interactions. One example could be ensuring that all staff take some time to themselves and create a healthy work/life balance.

Continue building a dependable framework for interactions and consultations to gain impressive results! The ability to communicate with positive outcomes in mind is crucial and has a profound impact on performance.

All staff members, including physicians, are happier and more productive with improved patient care and rising financial metrics!

You have worked hard to establishing yourself. Take that foundation of knowledge to strengthen your role as a community leader and businessperson … and take that vacation!

We ask in this volume about the drive that keeps us ever faithful to improving patient care. What keeps us here? Administrators often bring a great energy and passion to their work. We may love our profession, but we have to maintain our sanity too!

One subjective and compelling answer: there are few industries more rewarding than healing people. It is hard to forget when we help someone heal or assist in managing a terminal diagnosis. Each one of us can make a huge difference in someone's life.

A friend of mine said one helpful goal is to offer each employee the opportunity to develop skills that address issues on *their* level. This allows staff to work collectively and independently, without the need for input. And most important, to break down barriers and help each staff member pursue what they never thought possible. What an amazing boss!

The Business of Caring: Balancing the Checkbook with Compassion

How do we keep compassion while creating policies and processes? This can be most certainly one of the most daunting parts of being an administrator and physician. Make no mistake about it, we are a business. To relay compassion while keeping the lights on is truly an art. Add to the challenge that managers are often powerless in controlling certain expenses, and the task seems even more daunting.

Controlling the cost of healthcare continues to be a challenge. For the past twenty-five years, as we have gone through managed care and other health initiatives to save money, we continue to be the number one nation in cost when comparing health expenditures of developed countries as a percentage of gross domestic product.

Due to heightened consumerism, a business is now also how patients view us, as just another commodity that can be replaced with a newer model!!! In a service where people may not be comfortable comparison shopping, sometimes we are seen similarly to any other service industry. But when they need us, they really need us … and as soon as possible.

Your practice will be compared to other practices that patients may or may not perceive offering the same services and purchase contingent upon their preference. It is now a competition along with compassion. The most important thing to remember is the power of your practice, and how your uniqueness is actively and visibly conveyed to staff, patients, and communities!

How can your practice express its individual value with a personalized meaning to prospective patients? Most of this is common sense. Having a giving heart and business savvy is certainly a great jumping-off point. Authenticity shows.

Many offices utilize their computer systems at a bare minimal level and do not go any further. They just do not have the time to explore function and capability. Now is the time. It is your job to make sure that all staff and physicians have the best and most current tools possible to do their job. Utilizing existing systems to their fullest potential is good business. Contact your vendors and dig deep. There are possibly many nuances and shortcuts that you are already paying for and can utilize now to save your staff time.

Let systems reporting support and point the practice towards the most fitting platforms. Our systems should work in tandem with operations resulting in a smooth workflow. There should not be work arounds.

What kinds of ethical standards are we setting for the future? Money or mission?

For sustainability, we have to analyze information in a way that helps us predict the maximum potential for a most progressive future. Some challenges remain timeless and some have seen solutions transitioning with generations of care.

In the early 2000s, the creation of a transformational massive data stream and unleashing that information was designed to offer predictability through measurement, which would allow practices to control outcomes more closely. Yet healthcare was erratic versus progressive in many venues. Have you ever known a time when it is not?

We are constantly moving, hopefully in a forward direction!

In the 2000s, some were correctly projecting that healthcare services would become more customer focused and personalized. I believe that it was due to managed care plans restricting patients to a fault. A patient could be in the same building, and just going through a different door would require another referral for it to be approved. Incredibly labor-intensive. Many patients were beyond unhappy and, coinciding with growing consumerism, were able to speak up and be heard by employers and insurers. The result has been insurance plans offering more opportunity for the patient to be a part of their healthcare decision-making.

It was also a time when leadership changed from responding to outside systems and community influences to anticipating what other entities may be doing. This also signaled for providers to be more involved and accountable for areas beyond direct patient care. For example, being more aware of computer systems, staffing, and other major decisions regarding financial and operational decisions.

Where Is Our Crystal Ball?

How can we best prepare for the next stage of our professional lives? Grandma always advised that no matter what you do, don't panic. One thing we know for sure is that people will continue to be sick and need help with sustaining their well-being. Think of long term rather than short term goals. Maintain a rapport with local professionals, read the newspaper, and watch the news. Keep an eye out for trends that are forming. Be the first to pick up on a new offering, anything that gives the practice an edge on the delivery of care for today's patient: access, convenience, locations, providers, and even staff!

When was the most recent time that you reviewed missions and goals with your staff? We are so busy putting out fires over the little details of daily life and getting a claim paid ... sometimes it helps to be reminded why we are here.

Is your staff aware of or even know your missions and goals? Are they only in your personnel manual?

Find opportunities to bring the mission of the practice to the fore. Consider a sort of branding for the practice. Post or place in communications to staff. The mission will set the standard that defines the quality of care—display it for staff to live what we would like to see!

If your mission statement does need refreshing, consider inviting your employees to be a part of the change. Encourage them to live by and help reframe the standards along with you. Staff will find new standards much easier to accept when they have been a part of the decision-making process that establishes those updated policies.

This personal investment from the staff turns into an organizational investment, and your patients will notice that.

Right now? Leadership can be on a scale from pure chance to 100 percent intentional. It's just like anything else. Here we are, now what? What do we do with the responsibility, the power, and a more than demanding schedule? Do we use our power for favoritism or a balanced and progressive practice? The administrator needs to balance financial issues, personal dynamics, and referee conflicts. It is our charge to pass on all we have learned through our own experience as well as what we have learned from others.

> *"The purpose of life is to discover your gift. The work of life is to develop it. The meaning of life is to give your gift away."*
>
> *David Viscott*

The World Is Your Oyster! Consider a Retreat for You and Your Staff

A retreat is not just about touchy-feely stuff. It includes business goals as well. Begin with and post your draft agenda. Invite staff to contribute. It is enlightening and cathartic and helps the practice move to the next step. A well-designed retreat clarifies and confirms standards and values you want in place and defines who will be there for the long run.

A few tips? Mandatory attendance including physicians. Always have food. No recording! Avoid the emotional triggers by having an independent, and I mean independent, facilitator. This can help level the playing field of objectivity and make it easier to guide the conversation to a productive answer.

Our future is what we make it. And it is up to us to determine what kind of future we want to conserve and build upon.

An example of how to use your experience at a personal level, try beginning with one person—offer to help decipher a friend's medical bills. We can confirm the validity of a medical bill within 30 seconds that would take them hours. It's a huge help since we know the lingo. You will be amazed at how much you can help in just a short time.

Story

From Dr. William Fink, a general practitioner and OB/GYN from Brooklyn, New York.

> My grandfather (Grandpa Bill) was a pharmacist who then completed his studies to become a physician. One story my father would often tell is how my grandfather was able to care for entire families of patients throughout times of financial hardship.
>
> And wanting to pay my grandfather's bill, patients often had a lot of pride, but no money. So, he would barter for services. My father remembers waking up several mornings to find baskets of eggs, apples or potatoes or freshly washed and ironed shirts stacked by the back door.

While we can't expect the practice to accept food in lieu of payment, we can bring this kind of mindset to our work and our day-to-day lives.

We are at the beginning of what can be a beautiful healthcare platform of care for us and our families' futures. We can be that one whisper (or scream) that starts the whole thing! Create the ripple that is the constant catalyst for change! A little consideration, a little thought for others, makes all the difference. We can set the example as we consistently clarify and realign new principles, while redefining selective ethics of care.

You, your heart, and your brain—that's the true business of medicine.

Healthcare *is* local. There's nothing closer than the physician and the patient in the room discussing something intensely personal. Nothing can replace that, and it should be well supported. Let us honor the profession and the patient—and do it well!

"Choose what you love, and you will never have to work a day in your life."

Unknown

3

Emotional Intelligence Essentials

Emotional Intelligence

Emotional intelligence is the "something" in each of us that is a bit intangible. At a personal level, it is being cognizant of our demeanor and natural instinctive behaviors. At a professional level, emotional intelligence allows an administrator to understand the dynamics of the office social structure and help everyone find their place in that structure. Emotional intelligence also teaches us approaches to engage staff, thus improving overall time of service performance and patient collections! Utilizing emotional intelligence also comes to bear as administrators navigate their relationships beyond the medical practice, allowing them to understand, assess, and maintain a rapport and rhythm with our patient that reflects confidence, accountability, and growth.

Emotional intelligence is made up of two primary competencies: personal competence and social competence, as well as four core skills that pair up suitably: self-awareness and self-management, and social awareness and relationship management.

Our skills in emotional intelligence impact how we manage behavior, navigate social complexities, and make personal decisions that achieve positive results. It's about us and the human relationships, rational and emotional, and how they all work together. It's about the heart and the mind and impacts everything we do and say.

In our offices, we constantly interact with co-workers about pleasant and unpleasant matters. Being mindful of verbal and nonverbal signs can help impact the experience in the most positive way. We can meet this by recognizing our emotional intelligence strengths and weaknesses and working to make sure our skills in this area meet the needs of both the patient and the practice.

The Physical Connections

The communication between your emotional and rational brains is the bodily source of emotional intelligence. There is a literal physical response and connection that occurs. The physical pathway for emotional intelligence originates at the spinal cord. Your primary senses enter here and must travel to the front of your brain before you can think rationally about your experience.

First, they travel through the limbic system, the place where emotions are generated. So, we have an emotional reaction to events before our rational mind is able to engage. Remember too that the deeper the emotion the more we need to think about it. Think of being in love or when you have been so angry about something you cannot let it go. You've got it. This is why our parents told us to count to ten.

Personal Awareness and Competence

Personal competence is your ability to stay aware of your emotions and manage your behavior and tendencies. This is comprised of self-awareness and self-management skills, which focus more on you individually than on your interactions with other people. That can be hard!

This is your ability to accurately perceive your emotions and stay aware of them as they happen.

Self-awareness is being able to work with instinctive feelings and internal impressions to help guide our decisions in an optimistic way. We can recognize and regulate how we react to cues and recognize "buttons" we have that others trigger. This is being aware of our personal limitations as much as what we may handle with ease. There is no right or wrong. It is simply the way we are.

This insight helps us maintain composure, gain confidence, and communicate in an assured and positive style.

We then further build self-worth and confidence with each educational opportunity and additional training, as we encourage ourselves to be continually motivated to learn.

Self-management is your ability to regulate your emotional state to stay flexible and in a more constructive flow. This also enables you to control impulsive feelings and managing your emotions in a self-controlled healthy manner.

This competence grants you the insight to recognize and seek opportunities that can help improve your ability to for fill your role and more.

Self-management is not just about avoiding blowing up at someone. Here are some examples to consider how self-management can impact dealing with patients. One opportunity is to have a beginning script or practiced conversations to help someone continue on an even keel … e.g., judiciously dealing with an upset patient. If the patient has a valid complaint, it's a matter of handling it in a diplomatic manner … or a patient that has already been pressing your buttons may awaken an internal bias that can place a large hurdle to remaining level. Emotional intelligence in instrumental in both interactions.

"As I have said, the first thing is to be honest with yourself. You can never have an impact on society if you have not changed yourself … Great peacemakers are all people of integrity, of honesty, but humility."

Nelson Mandela

To strengthen self-management and control, ponder potential exchanges when working with various individuals and your willingness to change ideas or perceptions based on someone else's understanding and novel ideas. Also observe when and how you are able to calmly and evenly handle multiple stressful demands at one time. We always want to strive to meet and improve the standard of excellence that we expect of ourselves.

Social Competence and Social Awareness

Social competence is a combination of your social awareness and relationship management skills. This enables us to understand and anticipate other people's behavior, needs, moods, and motives in order to improve the quality of your relationships. We are also more comfortable in recognizing dynamics in social settings. It helps leverage and work to each person's strengths when cultivating opportunities for each staff member.

Social awareness is your ability to accurately pick up on emotions in other people and understand what is *really* going on. This perception allows you to understand unspoken and partially expressed thoughts and feelings.

As you read this volume please think about your entire office, every staff member, every room and corner. Ponder the atmosphere, employees, noise level, and anything that can affect an employee's communication and actions when relaying or requesting information for patients or co-workers. That's everything, right? So let's filter the perception a little bit.

Group and Organizational Awareness

Group and organizational awareness, in the context of emotional intelligence, helps us handle practice culture, dynamics, and hierarchy. Understanding who influences who. We recognize the values and how it affects our behavior. As leaders, we work hard and attend to the tasks at hand. We are influencers that always have plans A-D.

An effective leader can recognize what patients, employees, and providers all need, and what can be met in a way that encourages overall higher performance. It's our job. We build stronger teams by strategically utilizing the emotional diversity of staff members to benefit the practice as a whole.

Relationship Management

This is the ability to use awareness of your and others' emotions to manage interactions successfully. For example, having a difficult conversation with a particularly challenging staff member or physician.

Along with conflict resolution, relationship management is also at play when we also inspire others and connect with peers.

Fine tune relationship management skills by focusing on being as diplomatic as possible when a difficult situation arises. Centering on the issue will help de-escalate a highly emotional situation as we address and resolve in a most positive manner.

Some key points to keep in mind:

- Turn anger into positive energy and see where you can go with it.
- Speak half as much as you listen.
- It is essential to acknowledge and be respectful to validate others' issues and feelings.
- The best way to show you authentically care is by building trust and displaying honest interest.
- Try to differentiate and distinguish between your feelings and your thoughts.

Keep in mind that emotional intelligence as a whole is not just about being sensitive; it's being aware of your feelings and the feelings of others around you. It is also being smart with your emotions. We truly incorporate the correlations between emotions and thoughts to fully experience each interaction. My friend Lynette would call it a "smart heart."

An example? What is the best approach for us to successfully pursue collection on an account when the patient is clearly upset? Let's add that they are throwing a fit at the front desk. How would we handle that?

This is where those scripts and role-playing can greatly ease into and assist in maintaining that even keel required to manage such a difficult situation while also making sure all staff are delivering the same message.

Self-awareness acknowledges what (or who) triggers your emotions. How can we recognize and stabilize our behavior? There are times when, perhaps having previously practiced conversations can help someone resolve a situation in an empathetic and positive manner, e.g., when dealing with a staff member that has a less then preferable performance review.

Of course, there are times when we cannot help but take it personally, especially when there is a patient screaming at us in the hallway. What we have to remember is that if it were not us standing there it would be someone else. To them, it is not personal; they would be angry at whoever was placed in front of them.

Self-management allows you to filter information and approach issues in a more intuitive personal way and then apply relationship management skills to address issues in a global manner.

Also consider a situation where a long-standing and excellent employee that did not receive the raise or promotion they felt they deserved and threatens to leave. How would you handle that? This is where the emotional intelligence kicks in, with no buttons pressed, promoting transparency and communication for a better practice-wide understanding for each employee as well as ourselves. Placing ourselves in their position and having an honest, candid, empathetic, and supportive conversation with a staff member can help forgo a lot of negative reactions and actions and maintain positive morale.

Give it five minutes and there will most likely be another instance—such as a provider wanting to know why it takes so long to get patients to the back and to inform you that the new schedule is not working!

Connections are not based on the time spent, but on the quality of the experience of that time together. Enable all employees to get to know your authentic personality, style, and, maybe most importantly, your leadership priorities.

We need to listen, be respectful, and accept ownership when things don't go the way we envisioned they would. Nothing shuts down communication faster than criticism and blame. While a leader wants to hold a leadership team responsible for results, they also want to know what obstacles may be inhibiting success. This may be the time to ask what could have been done better to position everyone for the best possible results.

One manager told me the most important thing that they can convey to staff is that each employee is expected to do their job … and how can I help you do it? Independence with 100 percent support! This clearly reflects a personal interest while holding staff members accountable, positioning their employees for success!

4

Hire First Class Staff—
And Hold On!

"Between stimulus and response there is a space. In that space is our power to choose our response. In our response lies our growth and our freedom."

Viktor E. Frankl

Recruiting Techniques

I have a literally recruited a staff member from a breakfast buffet. Sometimes you can just sense it, right? While eating breakfast, I could not help but notice this one person taking extra steps and initiative in their role. They were very friendly to the customers and had a very pleasant attitude. Isn't that a great place to start? You can teach tasks, but initiative is a natural characteristic that we could always use more of! Another incredible staff member was discovered at a donut shop. This person was so clearly beyond competent and happy to please the customer. They went above and beyond in a helpful way to staff and customers. Initiative is a beautiful thing.

Where are the best places to advertise? Within arm's length and online. Depending upon the position, tap into the most current trending online listings along with local, state, and national medical manager forums. You may implement finder's fees for staff member referrals or post on a local social media page. List serves, professional specialty, and medical societies are other options. You will find what works best for you and your practice.

Job Postings

We had just set up some beautiful new diagnostic equipment and needed to hire someone to manage this new department and perform testing. For some reason, we had less than stellar applicants and time was getting tight.

I placed an ad similar to an invitation with an impactful headline highlighting the practice mission, events, and community support we provide. I added more specifics about the role and promoted our local awards and pride in our staff. I considered the position from a "wouldn't it be great to work here?" approach. This approach resulted in much better candidates.

Transparency works greatly to your benefit. Always provide as many details in the listing with as much of the job description as you are comfortable sharing publicly. Ponder how frustrating it can be for any candidate to apply to who knows where? I think it's more than reasonable for an applicant to at least know who they are applying to and the specialty. This allows the applicant to be more specific as to your particular opening. As we all know, a family practice is very different than an oncology or physical therapy setting. This helps filter the responses as possible contenders self-select for a role they would really want.

This is the perfect opportunity to identify your practice with pride! Promote those perks when appropriate. Your own baseball team, excellent annual celebration, or even cookies at three! Why not? Any applicant wants to envision going to a job they enjoy.

By the way, from describing a great practice and team, the most incredible and perfectly qualified person applied and is running the department to this day.

Scrutinize Resumes

As resumes are reviewed, check references, and I strongly suggest you do not rely upon the phone numbers or emails made available. Look the reference up yourself so you may confirm you are really speaking with the reference and not a friend of the prospective employee. I once contacted a reference where the "supervisor" turned out to be the applicant's boyfriend. And I almost did not catch it! References should also be supervisors or above, not co-workers.

Look for inconsistencies and make sure everything matches and makes sense. Applicants sometimes try to cover a questionable past by stretching the dates of more favorable employments and projects.

Ask previous employers for information along the lines that the applicant shared and compare the answer with what is on the resume. Also confirm exact dates of employment with references.

Please investigate any reservations you may have. It is good to pay attention to our instincts.

Perform a background check on all employees regardless of past or present relationships with staff. However, it is important to note that many employees who ultimately were found to have embezzled from a practice had no history of criminal activity.

For our physicians, recognizing the importance of emotional intelligence when hiring is key from a physician's point of view, especially with managers. This is a most important relationship where we must feel comfortable in communicating and making crucial decisions together, where there may be some respectful disagreements along the way.

Without realizing it, we are most often the main conduit of the practice culture. We take in everything from everybody and then process into the most productive result possible! Mindful physicians work accordingly and in correlation with managers and what is best for the patient care is determined as joint decisions.

Other than the patient, the physician is the central focus and should be involved on some level with all hiring and confirm approval of management hires and any other staff positions deemed suitable.

In turn, as a physician, with newly hired staff and anytime possible, a personalized introduction and welcome is always a most impressive and positive move. All it takes is eye to eye contact, a handshake, and a sincere welcome to the practice to promote loyalty from day one!

The Interview

"Words mean more than what is set down on paper. It takes the human voice to infuse them with deeper meaning."

Maya Angelou

As important as it is that we decide who we would like to speak with, it is just as important to select a comfortable setting for candidates during the interview ... coffee, water, even donuts! (Yes, I love donuts). Allow the applicant to see the interview as a warm welcome instead of an interrogation. It's amazing how "breaking bread" can make someone feel a little less held back, and you will want people to offer information freely as soon as possible. The goal is for the applicant to speak 80 percent and the interviewer to speak 20 percent of the time.

The job description can serve as the introductory template of the job. As you inquire about and discuss specific points, a candidate with experience should be able to fill in the blanks so to speak ... the between the lines details.

Consider opening with a "comfort level" category on interview templates. This is strictly a simple reaction that I have numbered levels one to five.

Ask individual and teamwork questions in as open-ended a way as possible. Make sure it is one that offers a chance for them to convey their demeanor (and hopefully) positive approach. Keep in mind that the questions are key to connecting. Here are a few suggested questions:

- What did you do to prepare for this interview?
- What have we not asked you about that you would like us to know?

- What is a good example of a team experience you found rewarding?

- As they answer, triangulate the response. Go a little deeper ... e.g. Why so? Tell me more ... What made that important to you? What steps made that actually happen?

As layers of anticipated questions are asked, I often find that the first answer is rehearsed, second tells a little more, and the third gives real insight. Two examples:

- Tell me about a time when you experienced failure and how you took that and changed the outcome.

- Tell me about a time when you worked with someone either at the same level as you or a different level and taught to them a new skill to help them grow.

A physician told me that they always ask themselves when hiring someone, "Who do you see sitting in that chair?" This reflects an effort to feel an initial instinctual impression to interviewees. And it works!

It takes only seconds to make a first, and usually lasting, impression.

Sometimes it's neutral and sometimes bells and whistles are going from all directions. I have learned to pay attention to my instincts.

Find time to "bump into" a physician during the interview. It is important and most respectful to at some point introduce any applicant you are considering hiring to a physician for a brief and initial impression. At my practice this is usually a pre-arranged, quick five-minute meeting for candidates that we are seriously considering hiring. Just as physicians diagnose a patient, using emotional intelligence during this time allows them to gain an initial impression and ask important questions. We are together eight hours a day or more and the more honest feedback we receive serves to strengthen us as we build our team.

Personality / Profiling / Testing

When you think about spending that much time a day with someone, it may not be a bad idea to find out a little bit more about them ahead of time. There are many tests that bring out an applicant's character, leadership qualities, fears, confidence, demeanor, and approach. Whether they are shy or assertive, bold or quiet, these elements can help you offer the office a sense of balance. Another consideration is that human behavior is complex and often depends upon our environment and our mental and biological states. There are limitations to how much you can really tell by spending thirty minutes with someone asking them questions they may have already been asked in previous interviews.

Demeanor is here to stay and only very rarely can be changed. It is a great advantage to be able to tap into what people are good at so that you may focus on their strengths from the first day of employment. It is great to be able to foresee and anticipate to better place people in the most appropriate positions. You can go with a tried and true character/personality assessment product or investigate the newest offerings. To find a product that fits your practice best, first determine what characteristics you would like to identify, for instance emotional intelligence, and go from there. For example, it is very easy to identify an extrovert utilizing the Myers-Briggs type indicator.

There are limitations to the scoring of tests that may disqualify an otherwise great candidate. Think about how a test may show someone as an extrovert but may not say who may be persistent. An employee with a good personality can be a lot of fun, however that does not necessarily mean they will be successful in the workplace.

Sometimes we can also go too far. We don't want to rule out what could be an exceptional employee because of a bad day. Trust your instincts. You never know and want to take hold of the best and brightest as soon as you see them!

The Stress Interview!

As we look at different kinds of interviews, it is important for this approach to be included as more of an example of an idea that may have gone too far and what not to do!

This experience is known as a *stress interview*, which tests how applicants deal with pressure.

This is done by taking them out of their comfort zone. An interviewer will ask a candidate a bizarre question such as "Why are manhole covers round?" Or ask them to complete an expected task on the spot, such as a cash flow projection or a white board presentation. The entire point of this kind of interview is to see how a candidate reacts to questions and what you may observe of their thought process when under pressure.

This could make sense with some jobs that are stressful. Strong questions are one thing, but there is a very big difference between asking a hard question and belittling the interviewee.

This method is mentioned also because you will not be the only one recruiting new staff members. Consider the candidate's first impression, as they are interviewing the practice as much as you are interviewing them, correct? We want it to be a good fit for all parties involved. What kind of impression will those interviewed leave with and relay to their friends or others considering working there too? Negativity is never a good way to start.

Team/Peer Interview?

There is a lot of merit to one's initial reactions and instincts to a candidate.

Peer interview? Yes, yes, and yes. We all know that the real getting things done lays with the team members. Maintaining an environmental balance is critical for the entire practice as well as subsets of care.

This introduction can be as long or as short as you would like, with as many employees as you prefer to include. The quickest team peer interview I can think of is to escort the candidate during the interview to the area where they may be working, so they may meet their prospective peers. After all, they are potential co-workers.

After familiarizing the interviewee with the area and staff, excuse yourself for a few moments. This allows your staff to ask some casual "getting to know you" as a potential co-worker questions to obtain a general feel for the candidate. You would be amazed how much your team will be able to tell in five minutes. Be sure to prep the staff with legalities, such as asking only work-related questions and not to ask any personal questions. Very simple and no pressure. Examples could be: What practices have you worked with? What systems have you used? And anything that relates to the position and feels comfortable in a professional forum. This is a perfect example of staff members tapping into most basic emotional intelligence as they are having a conversation. Remember impressions are made in twelve seconds. Listening to staff feedback after these team interviews has paid off for me every time.

If appropriate and possible, it is also good to try to catch another manager, even for just a few moments, to get their input as well. At this point you are gathering information and there is no such thing as too much, especially when you're going to be spending around forty hours a week with them!

Emotional Intelligence and Interviewing Approaches

There are many benefits to understanding how the emotional intelligence quotient plays into each step of the recruitment process that easily carry over into daily interactions, reduced turnover, higher quality of care, increased employee satisfaction, and identifying leadership characteristics.

Ascertaining the applicant's aptitude for self and social awareness truly helps us easier find the applicants who have a natural compassion and a devotion to their individual role as well as recognizing and fitting into the many tangents of interdepartmental communications. You will also want someone who inspires and brings out the best in themselves and those around them. Yes, we want it all. Why not? And if we go for it, we can come very close at times!

One of the best ways to find out about an applicant's emotional intelligence skills is an honest, well worded and thought out question without too many details. Keep the deeper questions to a minimum and spread throughout the interview. To get started, here are some examples and questions to pose that may offer an insight as to the candidate's capabilities and potential related to emotional intelligence:

- Has there been a conversation or event when you had to remain calm under tremendous pressure?

- How do you respond to someone that has an idea you do not like or know it will not work?

- Was there ever someone you worked with that you did not get along with? Did you try to speak with them or improve the relationship? How did you do it?

- Can you tell us about a time when you would have to lead by example?

- In retrospect, did you ever make a decision that you later regretted? Did you try to resolve the matter?

- Can you think of an example of persisting through a challenging situation?

- On an average day, what percentage of time do you spend on people?

And as you are considering these questions, don't forget to pay attention to the total picture. Body language will sometimes convey just the opposite of what they are saying.

Realize that clinical competencies are no longer enough in a time when patient experience, population health, team-based care, and community initiatives are becoming more integrated into the medical practice. Identifying candidates with high emotional intelligence is one way you can build stronger teams. A compelling argument is that when interviewees are screened for emotional intelligence factors, companies experience a lower turnover in personnel. For example, a large metropolitan hospital reduced the critical care nursing turnover from 65 percent to 15 percent within 18 months of implementing an emotional intelligence screening assessment.[7]

With or without screenings, it is a perfect time to utilize our instincts and our own emotional intelligence to help us determine the best candidates for our specific patient base and practice culture.

According to a MGMAStat, 69 percent of healthcare leaders hire for a cultural fit, followed by 13 percent basing it on previous experience. Technical competencies and other skills were prioritized below these characteristics. The survey results also included that 40 percent of the respondents felt that communication is the most important factor for positive organizational culture. [8]

If for no other reason, think about the cost of replacing a staff member. Employee Benefit News shared Work Institute's 2017 Retention Report conclusion that it costs employers 33 percent of a worker's annual salary to hire a replacement if that worker leaves. So, the calculation for an employee making around $44,500 would be $15,000. A Willis Tower Watson survey suggested employers consider that their best investment was in creating a workspace that the best hires would want to work in rather than choosing people that fit the existing workplace. Also keep in mind that having a lack of a path for career development is likely to create dissatisfaction on the job. Most employees stay for two years before seeking another position. [9]

Beyond the cost of replacing an employee is also the expense of reduced productivity and possible overtime hours for those who are filling in until the new position is filled. Consider your turnover and think about how often this is occurring as it can rapidly affect morale.

If you would like to know where your practice stands, you can determine your turnover rate. Divide total terminations by your average number of employees and multiply the answer by 100 to convert to a percentage. Suppose you lost 33 employees over the last 12 months out of an average workforce of 110. Divide 33 by 110 then multiply by 100 to find the employee turnover rate of 30 percent.

Total terminations ÷ Number of employees x 100
= Turnover rate

33/110 * 100 = 30%.

According to DailyPay, healthcare turnover rates have risen 5 percent over the last decade. Depending upon your region in the country turnover for facilities can be anywhere from 16 to 19.5 percent.[10] If you are higher than that, look at possible reasons why and how to improve staff retention in the future. Comparing with practices within the region will offer a recent comparison to most local peers. Of course, utilizing state and national specialty societies only adds to the information that can help as we update most fair recruiting and personnel policies.

A Job Well Done!
Awards and Rewards

We've done it! We've hired the absolutely best people. Now what? There are times when we can be shortsighted without realizing it. For example, we may spend thousands to recruit someone and then not approve funding for a birthday gift basket.

There is absolutely nothing wrong with letting someone know they have done a stellar job! Why not? There are times we cannot see how good an employee is until they leave. Retain the best by letting them know they are appreciated. Especially in shaky times, we want to reinforce those most valued.

So, close your eyes and envision your employees … think about who has done something above and beyond their station that should be acknowledged. Why wait? It's always good to reward and incentivize initiative. These are the people you want to keep as your staff members, right?

No consequences or rewards result in a stagnant workforce with no motivation. Truly, why should I work hard when my co-worker does not, and *they* get a raise!

Rewards can be simple. For example, a friend of mine inherited a practice that had very low morale and a general disinterest in any kind of meeting. She began to hold raffles at each meeting. They were thoughtful prizes that did not cost a fortune and were a nice little bonus. Engagement and initiative increased, and she helped them grow to become an incredible dedicated team.

When you show authenticity in your concern for staff and the practice on a daily level with little and big events and issues, your staff notices!

I have a question for you. What avenues have you created so employees feel seen, heard, and recognized? Devoted and loyal staff are worth their weight in gold!

- ◆ Worried about longevity? Offer an anniversary day celebration. (longevity = saving rehiring money).

- ◆ Bonus/reward? Make it personal! Avoid redundancy and personalize each gift by utilizing apps and human resources (HR) platforms that help you get to "know" if an employee would prefer movie tickets or a massage.

- ◆ For a special break? Timing is everything. One staff member may prefer a fifteen-minute break each morning and another may need the third Tuesday of each month to volunteer. If the role allows, meeting personal desires allows them to lead the life they choose, and why then, would they seek another job?

Use Emotional Intelligence to Take Each Employee's Emotional Temperature

There will be times when staff will not tell you things that you need to know for a million reasons ranging from peer pressure, to being too personal, simply preferring not to. This is why it is so important to design opportunities that allow each person to anonymously express how they honestly feel about the practice atmosphere. It may be preferable to have an independent person or vendor perform a study that asks questions that clearly reflect a candid view that can help assess your staff member's morale. There are many things that will be confirmed and even possibly previously approached and time for a refresher course! Remember too that any gathering of information also confirms the positive and productive things as well. This helps with staff retention as your best staff may leave due to unaddressed or unresolved issues because they can find a job anywhere!

Think about the following as a good starter for questions. A respondent should not take any more than 10 to 12 minutes of their time on this.

What kind of emotions do you feel at work?

(Please circle the top 5 that apply)

Stressed

Happy

Frustrated

Motivated

Resentful

Confident

Angry

Depleted

Satisfied

Depressed

Compassionate

Sad

Nervous

Tired

Lucky

Worried

Content

How do you feel about your work in relation to your capabilities?

(Please circle top 3 that apply)

Matched to qualifications.

Love my job.

Hopeful it will balance out.

Here for the benefits, not the position.

Need more training to get the job done.

Have many things to offer if asked.

Overqualified for my post.

Overwhelming.

A good balance.

Energizes me.

Would like to change positions.

How do you feel about leadership?

(Please circle top 4 that apply)

My boss is not at all effective.

My supervisor inspires me.

I trust my manager.

I am invisible.

I feel heard.

I am afraid to speak up.

My boss listens to me.

I don't even know who my boss is.

We need more time to meet.

Our meetings are productive.

They talk and I listen.

And follow up questions such as:

What can your manager do to reflect awareness of your role and value?

Is there something the practice leaders can do that could show their support to uphold a more positive morale?

What activities or events do you think could help with honoring or displaying staff member support?

What are you grateful for?

What would you change?

The next step, if not already, is to take action. Staff will be waiting and watching for some changes following. Invite all to be a part of these new events and processes. This is a great transparency opportunity and promotes staff engagement, helping create "the change they would like to see!" I love win-win situations.

> *"I am always doing what I cannot do yet in order to learn how to do it."*
>
> *Vincent Van Gogh*

Emotional Intelligence and Personnel Policies

We cannot assume that bad things aren't happening just because our staff does not tell us about them. To be present when we are not physically there, an emotionally intelligent establishment builds in personnel policies that proactively support those who may be grappling with the loss of a loved one, depression, anxiety, or other issues. Please review and refine policies with the most empathy possible. Valued employees reciprocate their appreciation. For example, my friend had a stellar employee that wanted to transition to part time to spend more time with their family. The request was granted, and the employee was so appreciative, they purchased a thank you gift for her. The employee is still there today and the thank you gift is much cherished.

Transgender and Identity Policies

With time sensitive policies, it is of course important to be absolutely current by checking your local, state, and federal guidelines.

To help staff gain an understanding of what is meant, include definitions like the below, which were resourced from the Transgender Law Center's *Model Transgender Employment Policy of 2019*:

Gender identity: A person's internal, deeply felt sense of being male, female, or something other or in between, regardless of the sex they were assigned at birth. Everyone has a gender identity.

Gender expression: An individual's characteristics and behaviors (such as appearance, dress, mannerisms, speech patterns, and social interactions) that may be perceived as masculine or feminine. [11]

A few recommended guidelines for this category cover transition plans especially regarding restroom and locker room accessibilities. Be sure to also cover health insurance, harassment, and dress code. We want every single staff member to be 100 percent protected and respected.

Bereavement Leave

According to Susan Bartel, a researcher at Maryville University of St. Louis:

> Allowing longer bereavement leave gives employees an opportunity to adjust slightly to a new way of life before having to reengage in the world at large. If they feel their grief is recognized and understood they are more likely to contribute to the organization even earlier than they could otherwise.[12]

Giving someone a buffer day can make all the difference in the world. This can directly impact their demeanor as they return to work if given a brief respite at home before returning to work.

Employee Assistance Program (EAP)

If you are able, it is a great opportunity to offer such a benefit. These can be set up internally for education, trainings, support groups, and individually based needs. Be transparent in extending these programs in the wide open so that fear or pride does not inhibit employees taking advantage of a great platform. Having managers remind and promote a culture of encouragement is a great example of relaying your appreciation of their hard work. This can also help energize an employee that may otherwise be afraid to take that first step towards being a great leader.

Employee Wellness Programs

Your employees can learn healthy habits and be rewarded for those those they are already involved in. Participants in employee wellness programs are encouraged to take steps to be well through education, challenges, social encouragement and rewards.

A complete employee wellness program can include health risk assessment, individual and group challenges, onsite gym or memberships (exercise is a great distraction from work and a real stress reducer!), fitness tracker integration, biometrics, reporting, wellness education, cooking classes, "good health" rewards and incentives! An effective wellness program is a good way for employers to reduce healthcare costs plus improve engagement, performance, and overall well-being.

Reading and Leading Your Employees

Staff members can work with confidence, initiative, and pride when the person they report to has then covered 100 percent plus! As an employee, this is more than freeing. My boss has my back! No fear! I can fly! My decisions are trusted and supported.

As a leader, this means helping shape and improve a daily environment where each staff member can perform their job 100 percent with all the tools they need.

Gain strength through unity. Help them feel a part of the healing. Every practice has its mission and goals and staff members need to be able to relate their particular role to how it helps with those ideals, values and standards.

For example, as an employee, how does my checking in a patient help the goals of the practice?

Well, that's an easy one. If the patient registration is a smooth one, they are seen in a timely manner and the patient has great communication with their physician because of the clear notes that you have left, that helps meet the mission of continued access to physicians and timely patient care. Let staff know how operations are impacted and improved such as refining practice flow by better scheduling. Let them feel the gain.

It means the world to be appreciated, and recognition helps employees on all levels be an active part of something bigger than themselves. Focus your energy each day by touching base with staff members even if during a daily walk-through. A smile and eye contact can go far in affirming one's value.

Everyone Has a Voice: Meetings

One thing that most employees say is that everyone should have a voice. A meeting is a perfect time for that to be modeled.

Some say that meetings are just inefficient time suckers when everyone's time is so important. What a waste! We have a captive audience where we can serve food and things like chocolate that make people happy. Maybe some good news about an exciting purchase or upgrade for the practice. Things can go in a very positive way.

Have standing meetings, at least monthly. Show courtesy to all attending by always beginning on time. We do not want resentment in the air before the meeting even starts.

Employees are obliged to listen to us all the time—this is their time to speak in an open forum rather than a hallway decision that may not be remembered or stick!

The best decisions can often be made sooner when agenda and materials are sent ahead of time to be reviewed (department updates?) and avoid wasted time playing catch up. Thoughtful, respectful, and specific questions can help all be a part of the end decision. It also helps us set expectations and boundaries for con-sideration and discussion. It may require a little more effort on the front end of preparation, but it is so helpful in guiding those most important and timely decision. This is also a chance to place your "footprint" and make your personal brand more visible.

Remember, those who do not feel heard may instead convey their insecurities to co-workers, which can spread throughout the office. We want the most positive energy out there.

Staff members need to know we will listen, or they will never approach us. There needs to be two-way communication built into the format. The best mutual commitments and conversations begin with a collective identification of the issues at hand and how to take care of them.

Promote active input from physicians and other staff in the office to maintain balance, flow, and respect for all departments. It can help spark some productive conversations.

This is also the perfect opportunity to stress the impact staff meetings can have. It does not matter how big or small your practice is, everyone should have an open forum to speak with other staff! They can't do it at the front desk while a patient is waiting to be checked in.

An employee needs to be able to look physicians (and you) directly in the eye and have a meaningful conversation about issues so everyone can work together and resolve them.

With a few key issues being discussed at general staff meetings with a temporary "let's try it for thirty days" method, and then addressed observations and/or results in a collaborative manner at the next meeting. Of course, we knew almost right away if it worked (or not), and more staff came up with ideas. Nothing like initiative! New ideas are brought up all the time with some working and others not. *That* is continual growth and progress.

Practice Hierarchy and Departmental Dynamics

Office Gossip

Favorites in anyone's book of management problems are office gossip and departmental dynamics. One thing about practice relationship issues is that they may be unaddressed for a long time and may be seen solely as part of the office gossip.

Don't let the good ones go! See Chapter 6 for how to incorporate "postural feedback" and incoporate it now!

It is understood and natural that there will always be a low level of gossip. To me, it is similar to stress. A little bit reminds you what's going on, with hints and actions that may or may not need to be taken. One example to mull over is when it grows and interferes with patient care and work processes.

Another thing to ask ourselves is how many good employees have left in the last year due to interpersonal issues or staff dynamics? The truth is that one way or another we end up addressing issues 99.9 percent of the time. All too often, it is after a great employee departs.

There is a saying that is appropriate for this kind of a situation. Nip it in the bud. It adds to your credibility when a problem is approached in the beginning with all parties involved. Protecting the practice is your highest priority.

Harmful, intimidating, or separative gossip can disintegrate morale and divide employees into cliques, which can gradually transition your practice culture into a downward spiral. Gossip, once out there, can linger for a long time before being forgotten. It is a weapon of influence. Gossiping can often involve manipulative behavior and is an instant morale killer.

If practice-wide improvements are needed, consider a department and/or practice-wide retreat or teambuilding communications seminar to improve interpersonal relationships and awareness. If the problem is more on an individual basis, then working with each person involved in the quietest and most respectful manner possible will hopefully reap improved behaviors.

Great leaders have the ability to maintain objectivity and avoid becoming too involved. To remain uninvolved in a gossipy conversation, remember what Maya Angelou said: "I'm not in it."

Here are some telling inquiries if conducting an interview or survey:

◆ Do you feel that gossip is too much a part of the office and practice culture?

- What are two things that you think would change the level of gossip?

- How often do team members pitch-in and help others beyond the scope of their own jobs?

- Are there just a few personalities on your team who provoke the gossip?

And a few ideas to help avoid gossip:

- Be brave. Bring it up directly and approach it honestly. You will be respected for it.

- Only speak about the people in the room as much as you can, and their words and behavior.

- Avoid mentioning those not present as the message may be misunderstood as well as incorrectly related.

There are a few ways to stop unneeded or harmful gossip in your office. Keep in mind that some people that gossip want to do it simply because they need to complain and appear helpless, at times playing the victim. If this approach works, the gossip tends to feed upon itself and just grows fiercer.

Choosing not to participate or "feed" the gossip weakens the gossiper's rewards. Just like feeding someone's anger sometimes just makes them angrier.

You can respond from a position of curiosity. One example could be, "What are you trying to accomplish by telling me this?" or "What would you do to change this?" or "I am curious, what are you asking me to do about this? Common sense responses can deflate their manipulation and diffuse the powerless factor.

It is amazing how much damage one person can do. Clear expectations as to behavior will sort out those that truly start things up and can be approached on an individual basis in specific places.

Secrets can fuel gossip. Be as transparent as possible about big and small projects, moves, and especially staff changes. Post statuses and forecasts of projects and calendar events for all to see, whether via systems or posting on the break room walls. It also directly invites and helps keep staff engaged in practice activities.

When you are recognized for resolving problems quickly, you are proactively supporting those who work hardest and endorse a healthy work environment. This is a true leader and great administrator!

We can only do so much. As said, gossip is a natural factor of life. It's how we deal with it and the settings of communication that make all the difference in the world with our practice's humanity and philosophies.

What Do Administrators Need? Resources, Respect and Support.

Administrators require encouragement and backing so they are visibly seen by all as the practice leader. Physicians are the best ones to bolster the administrator's role and authority. Respect of course is a two-way street. Your employees (using their emotional intelligence) can tell when ideas and new policies are presented in a united manner, and that's when the loyalty factor kicks in!

Professional Certifications that Affirm Leadership

We can always benefit from more education and training at any time. One way to put your already gained knowledge on paper for others to recognize is by attaining a professional certification. Fortunately, there are a plethora of choices through many different entities depending upon specific factors. For instance, you may choose to focus on total management, coding, specialty, hospital, or more private practice-oriented specialties. There are many certifications that affirm professionalism offering invaluable additional knowledge. One often unanticipated bonus will be the incredible relationships formed along the way. College degrees are a wonderful thing but can become dated. Professional certifications keep you on a more current basis and in tune with the most recent requirements and trends.

There are managers who do not grant themselves enough credit for their own life education and wisdom. Medical administration is a gradually built and indispensable knowledge that can only be fully gained from experience. This exceptional "in between the lines" understanding of issues reflects valuable, constructive, and creative cognitive decision-making with most positive results.

Professional certifications are beyond an investment in your future, and they will benefit your practice as well. Check with the appropriate specialty organizations as well as medical manager groups and any professional affiliation that helps move you forward as well as affirm your experience and expertise. You can pursue as many as you want. It will only make you better. Invest in yourself—and not just the education, invest in your life's future. Treasured relationships build your health and stamina. Take care of all of you.

Staff Training and Continuing Education

Does each and every staff member have what they need to complete their role?

Staff training can be instantly worthwhile! Whether it be an in-house or conference setting, it pays for itself. Have someone work and train with collections, billing, and front desk staff, and you will see your staff members' workflow soar! You may choose to have a workshop internally to either approach a problem that you would rather keep within the practice or to develop a truly 100 percent customized program specifically for your office that you can record for new employees down the road to view as well.

Emotional intelligence is "the capacity to be aware of, control, and express one's emotions, and to handle interpersonal relationships judiciously and empathetically."[13] It is managing your relationships and awareness in a positive and empathetic direction … tapping into your instincts while being aware of your actions and managing relationships in a constructive direction. A great example of a win-win training program for you and your staff would be focusing on emotional intelligence. Even just a half-day workshop will pay for itself each time one of the team has a productive and helpful interaction with staff, patients, or physician.

Those who are trained in emotional intelligence perform at a substantially higher level than those who are not. Providing this sort of training also shows your staff you believe in and choose to invest in them. Educating all staff members at the same time promotes unity and helps codify updates to policies and procedures so all employees are relaying identical information. This creates a personal, organizational, and unified approach.

The Future of Our Work Is Creative

Taken as a whole, your staff members are professionals who want their abilities and skills to be used to the ultimate potential. We all want our best and most unique talents to shine and be recognized!

We also want to build an aware and high-performance team where being creative also means thinking about fringe ideas. These can at times be risky but that is also their strength, and when it works it is remarkable! It also stands a better chance of being noticed because it is so different.

Our patients rely upon us to offer the most up to date technologies and connections with information that can affect their lives. We want each staff member to communicate with patients in the most impactful and engaging way, at every level of care.

Change can take longer for some than others, especially when they have already established core assumptions and traditional values. We can blend the best of both. The great counterpart is that we are able to support forward thinking that is positive, which helps engage patients and staff members as we gain professional growth.

Thinking about the message that we choose to relay when we ask a staff member to complete a task can make a big difference! For example, "We have to collect more or there may not be any raises this year," compared to, "If we are able to collect at least 80 percent of our goal, we will probably get good raises!" Let your goals become theirs in an upbeat way.

One manager continually sets the goal based upon the best employees, so they continue to improve. Staff members become more invested when it's more personal.

There's nothing wrong with a little incentive that takes someone a step further. It also may help some in realizing they can do more.

One physician said to me that no matter the commission percentage, the practice typically recognizes more income than may have originally been anticipated. That makes sense!

Hold that carrot out! Invite, and many will go for it! We like bonuses for performance, why not others too? Adding healthy competition helps keep the momentum going. And when given the choice, people usually select reward over repercussion.

Staying Positive

We have all heard and possibly received the well-meant advice to "remain positive." Sometimes this kind of an outlook is simply unattainable, which can make it feel even harder to focus on a more positive outlook.

Another challenge is that our brains are hardwired for survival, a characteristic carried over from when we were hunters and gatherers. This adds fear to the equation.

To reduce the barriers of caution, look for opportunities to create less typical combinations of people.

For example, when you have meetings, consider asking staff to sit with employees from different departments (a must for retreats too)! Another example could be committees that are built with representatives from each department.

As I said earlier in this chapter, I don't think there's any other way to relax people more than "breaking bread" together. This is especially a good way to have employees feel welcome and unwind in a short period of time. There is something about it that makes you relax just a little bit. It also possibly leaves us a bit more open too.

An important element of remaining positive is promoting self-awareness where staff is able to direct their own path that can bring out their best in their career. Even when everyone is stressed, the positive energy exuded and shared lends to a more positive environment.

Living "in the moment" can also be a good thing to keep front and center in your mind. We often tend to focus and worry about the past, regrets about what should have been said, which leads to stressing about the future. It's true that there is absolutely nothing we can do about the past. Remember that any energy used to focus on the past takes away drive for and towards your future. Let it go and live in the moment.

Even with momentary benefits, we also must remember the long-term advantages. Positive emotions are often associated with improvement in performance, quality, and customer service. That is a great investment in your practice's future.

Being in the present can become a habit that helps you to move forward and will uphold an encouraging and creative environment that allows you to fine tune your awareness even further in the most beneficial way!

5

Emotional Intelligence and Resiliency in Times of Confusion

"In times of stress, the best thing we can do for each other is to listen with our ears and our hearts and to be assured that our questions are just as important as our answers."

Fred Rogers (Mr. Rogers)

We have all dealt with disasters at some point in our professional career. It could be an internal issue, emergent weather such as hurricane, tornado or flooding, and other natural disasters, as well as a crisis, including a worldwide or pandemic!

We experience fear, pressure, stress, and anxiety, and any one of those alone can be overwhelming. While it is our role in a professional setting to care for others, we also, of course, have to think about ourselves in order to maintain a routine and a level of sanity while providing patient care.

There is never a better time to be in tune with your staff and physicians. Emotional intelligence offers the familiarity needed and is the best way to respond to any emergency successfully.

Emotional Intelligence and Crisis Support

In volatile times, help staff be aware of their stress level so they may have more control of their emotions and are cognizant of others' emotions as well. There will be potential for, and experiences of, depression, burn out, and possible substance abuse. We can address these by guiding efforts and energies in more productive ways. It is also okay for your staff to see you being human. Allow them to offer their empathy and bond with you as the whole office approaches this together with empathy and transparency. We are all fearful and all have insecurities that need to be buffered. It's only natural to be distressed in such circumstances.

Our brain feels before it thinks. And, as many have learned, tensions are typically high throughout the practice. It is our job to help all stay calm, remaining positive while listening, diffusing tense situations and remaining grounded.

Be aware of the unspoken cues, the body language as you direct and work together. Do they offer confirming nods or look away and towards each other questioningly? Reassurance is elemental. Address any anticipated concerns. Remember too that people say stressful things in stressful times when everyone is at a fever pitch.

Try to respond instead of reacting. Managers are used to putting out fires every day and that thorough methodical thinking certainly assists in the ability in arriving at a well thought out solution. This of course is a more emergent and encompassing issue where touching base with all of your professionals, liability carriers, attorneys, and payers ahead of time can help you be more prepared.

Going through an uncertain time can actually be a very good bonding experience between staff members. Sometimes when people go through a very difficult life experience, they emerge from it with an incredible strength and resilience, and it may re-establish strained relationships. It is our job to balance all of these emotions and experiences.

When Unexpected

When chaos and confusion surround us, we want to avoid the unknown, the unclear. It is essential that leaders provide clear and consistent information. It is the role where you will have the most impact on success. Have a plan before you have a plan. Being process oriented, there is probably an already established disaster plan. That is the best place to start. Propose the situation where you cannot contact one person. Who would be the next one that can carry out tasks and/or delegate further?

Consider different resources when you anticipate different situations and possible shortages. Fear for our safety and health is worth addressing ahead of time. Create online templates of provisional care and recovery and supply that can be accessed by all staff and physicians.

It is also unfortunately true that we typically may not have contingency plans for other unanticipated tragic events, such as a staff member's death.

We had an incredibly valued and loved patient account manager that I said goodbye to on Friday, and then I had to say goodbye again (this time forever) on Monday at the hospital. It was an absolutely horrible time. We all took turns going to the hospital to see her, not even knowing if she was aware of us.

I remember at one point being in my office when the lead physician entered my office, closed the door and sat down, quite upset. I asked him what was wrong and how I could help him. He said, "It's really hard for me today when someone complains about a pimple on their arm, and Valerie is dying in the hospital." He sat quietly for a few additional moments and then returned to patient care.

The entire office was affected, and patients even noticed, asking, "Your staff is usually so happy, is there something going on?" We simply explained that we had experienced a death in the family. What held us together is what always holds us together. We share in healing and treating patients and there is no industry like it. We support each other with empathy and understanding, allowing us each our own time to get back to normalcy.

We may also have to isolate from our families during this time. Clinicians especially may be subject to remain-at-home orders in their off hours and have to consider the time that is spent away from their families and loved ones.

There also may be some employees that will need to be redeployed. This cannot only be traumatizing for the practice due to the staff members absence, but also bring additional stress to those being redeployed. Allow a transition period upon return. Redeployment should also be addressed in your personnel manual.

There may be times when additional help such as a psychologist or other resources can be offered and available for staff as they need in trying times. This affords each employee privacy as you convey support and show you value their well-being through any disaster. Be truthful. This is essential for trust. The scariest times are when we do not know how it may end. This approaches our most basic instinct of survival to which we can only do as much as humanly possible in anticipating and every possible scenario. Reduce the fear and deal with facts. Cover each department and each staff member's role. Don't have just plan A and B, but plan A, B, C, and D. Nobody is ever 100 percent prepared, but you should do as much as you can to expect the unexpected.

When You Know It's Coming: Preparing and Delegation of Responsibilities

In a perfect case scenario, we will know the answer when someone presents with that question, "What do we do now?"

If you have ever experienced any kind of disaster recovery, the second-best way to prepare for the next one is a debriefing afterwards while the memory is fresh. Ask managers to make notes as they can during the restoration as we tend to forget little details that can make a huge difference.

The best way of course is to have an amazing disaster and recovery plan that is developed by people who have actually experienced it. This is where geographical and professional list serves can greatly assist in ensuring we are able to include every element that can assist serving patients. We all benefit from being aware of additional resources and hopefully a quicker recoupment to complete patient care.

Obtain the physician's or board's approval as appropriate and have a comprehensive staff training when they are paying attention! This is important. It's also a great time as you review the plan for those who are carrying out responsibilities to stand and identify themselves. You may discover an even smoother way to proceed.

We can't be everything to everyone and delegating appropriately can relieve a great deal of pressure. Some staff members may be eager to do more as they may want to contribute as much as they can during a crisis. It's great to have a staff member with a mission. It's also good to remember that everyone has limits.

Emotional intelligence will help identify applicable boundaries as you establish who does what. Being aware of our own and others' limitations is essential in an emergency situation. If one person does not carry through, it affects everyone else in a crisis, and there is no time to make up for any mistakes. This is where experience counts. Review these plans quarterly to ensure that tasks are assigned to most current staff members and are appropriate according to their level and expertise.

As you may be considering remote workers, be sure to have your asset lists up to date and offsite worker agreements signed. If you are using an HR platform, be sure to have laptops and other equipment clearly designated to specific employees so they are easier to track.

Emotional intelligence kicks in during challenging times, offering the capacity to assign appropriate actions as we access and merge our emotions with reason, which results in intelligent and empathetic resolutions. The ability to discern others' emotions enables us to make better educated decisions. It is the role of the leader to drive their motivation towards results-oriented actions that may be needed even when additional or different than their daily routine. We also have to remember that to maintain an even keel, we control what we are able to and realize that we cannot control everything.

It can also be challenging as a leader as we are trying to run a business to also be aware that each staff member has a personal life to protect as well. We have to be sure to convey understanding of their situation and empathize throughout the ordeal. There are truly times when we are all in this together and there are many ways to work things out.

One idea towards being totally transparent is to have everyone in a meeting together discussing their specific needs and issues and working out schedules to maintain seamless patient care while addressing any personal situations that may also need to be addressed. Sometimes it's more complicated than that and sometimes it can be that simple.

One example is virtual visits. You will need to check with your liability carrier and confirm which states you are allowed to offer patient care and any situation based additional allowances. Also consider if you will be covered for new or only established patients during critical times.

If it is a health epidemic, which staff members may need to go home? Who may be at risk? That is a time to rethink priorities: over 60, pregnant, immune-compromised?

Staff: Maintaining While Providing

It is normal to feel unsettled when our world is suddenly thrown upside down. We can feel frozen in time and somewhat incapacitated. It is almost like shell shock … until we walk into the office … and then immediately start playing that role. It is our self-awareness that will help us recognize when we do things such as tightening our jaw or have stress in our voice, or perhaps we are breathing a little bit differently. Stay in touch with yourself as much as others.

When a disaster strikes, staff's personal lives can have drastically changed literally overnight, and we could all be dealing with a new reality of no power, water, or worse. Fears and emotional roller coasters may occur. Our goal is to project a predictable future and that we *can* get through this.

I learned after a major hurricane that our staff needs some TLC and assistance too! I contacted a therapist who spoke with staff about how to stay controlled, calm, and grounded. It was good to be able to proactively address rather than avoid individual and practice-wide fears. This is a good way for leaders to express excellent relationship management.

Assuming that some may not have power at their homes, such as after a hurricane, and other issues that could occur, try to make it a little easier while at the office. Put your empathy to work and try to provide a few extras to help employees get through tough times while they work so hard for the practice. Try to provide lunch every day, and chocolate *always* helps! Science has shown that good nutrition is directly linked to emotional well-being, which we all need during such times. And everyone knows chocolate is one of the basic emotional food groups!

In inclement weather, consider helping coordinate having a staff member that can pick up other employees, or carpooling that can save co-workers time and money as they are able to report to work.

This is an okay time to over communicate, as staying in touch and tuned in is vitally important to keep everyone going. It also enables us to anticipate how our staff members may react to certain situations or issues as they arise. Not clearly relaying extra efforts to be in touch with each employee (and their challenges during this time), can send inappropriate messages and flip to a very negative impact as staff members may perceive this as a lack of understanding.

Allow these times, when opportunities arise for face-to-face communications, to naturally encourage co-workers to relate and bond. Even brief conversations can help us reconnect in the mist of chaos, and that can energize us. No one is more aware of the stress we are experiencing than another co-worker. Good emotional intelligence is being aware of yourself and others around you. There is no better example than everyone rallying around handling an emergency situation together with respect and courtesy towards others.

A great example of how we can support our employees throughout comes from Lisa Bailey of Garey Orthopedics, who posted this on LinkedIn:

> Emotional intelligence. Let's have a brief discussion on the importance of being aware and present during this crucial time! As a millennial healthcare leader, I am aware that my team is stricken with fear because of the uncertainties that many of us are faced with.

I am aware that my team needs to be led with facts, a strategic recovery plan and over communication to provide that level of comfort to the unknown. I am aware that my docs need to be led with innovative technological advances, recovery strategies, strategic partnerships that create a circle of support, and, most importantly, aware of how the unknown is emotionally affecting them! During these times as leaders it is important to nurture your emotional intelligence so you can show up as the best version of yourself today! As an advocate for small businesses, an epidemic like COVID-19 can be detrimental. Being aware and present allows me to lead, mentor, and support my team effectively! I encourage all my millennial healthcare executives to lead present and aware in their roles, especially during this time of crisis. Create a circle of support with your peers. We are stronger together!

#healthcareprofessionals #millennial #strongertogether [14]

As a staff member under this administrator, I would feel totally secure that my leadership has a clear vision and positive answers that value and support my position within the practice. Thank you!

Physicians and Providers: Continuing Care

Support staff is just that. We run circles so patients may have the most impactful visit and be seen in the most caring way possible. With any developing emergency situation, always have at least one lead physician designated to be able to make determinations and approve decisions as necessary. Then, of course, have someone as a back-up in case the first provider is not available.

Patients with urgent needs are typically the first priority. If you know what is coming, for instance if a hurricane is forecast, we know how important it is as a first step to review the schedule in the lead time you have to anticipate needs and reschedule as you see most appropriate.

There is no such thing as being too prepared and patients will notice that as well. If your office seems chaotic during a chaotic time, it only heightens patients fear and negative anticipations. Remember the patients hear much more than you think. Keep an eye (and ear!) out for hallway conversations that should be held behind closed doors, a critical concern that can get lost in a rush.

I was walking down a hallway of a practice shortly after a hurricane, just after the power had come back on. There was a physician at the end of the hallway repairing a hydraulic door. I had to ask him to step down immediately, explaining to him that his hands were incredibly important and valuable, and that there were others who could fix the door. Everyone wants to help, but not everyone makes the most practical decisions in crucial times, so be prepared to be that level of protection. As leaders, administrators are the central resource correlating patient (and staff!) care as smoothly as possible.

Some examples that your staff (and you) can appreciate

- Extend paid leave for all staff, including part-timers. A little bit can go along way!

- Allow for casual dress whenever and wherever appropriate, especially if not seeing patients.

- Have leaders of the practice, typically the leading physician and the administrator, address the staff to offer guidance and support with total transparency—basically a motivational talk. You will actually be able to see your staff relax as the personal message is delivered. Like patients, staff also want to be cared for in stressful times.

- Keep an eye out for employee conflicts growing from the high stress, as it is likely some tempers may rise.

- Be prepared to refer challenged staff members to any employee assistance programs or some kind of mental health services that may offer confidentiality and serve the staff member further in managing the stress and the situation at hand.

We can all reduce the fear with the careful application of emotional intelligence. A great example of this was when some physicians working at Sharon Hospital in Petah Tikva, Israel, placed pictures of themselves on their protection suits so that patients suffering from infections of the novel coronavirus could see who was taking care of them. These physicians worked with staff members to reduce the fear patients were experiencing from the sight of providers fully suited up in PPE. Isn't it wonderful how human-level care and concern rules even in the middle of a pandemic?

And what to do afterwards? When you feel it is safe to approach, hindsight is always 20/20, conduct a full review with representatives from each department while the memory is fresh. As you work on the emergency plan revision, be sure to include all perspectives and ask for input and review from all participants to assess for any missing factors or important notes to remember. Little details count a lot in this sort of situation and hopefully save a lot of time in the future as you reformat your plan (that you will hopefully never have to use again). It can also help everyone access their best emotionally intelligent state to process what happened and what could be better together. Each of these elements of care is interwoven into components and foundational operations throughout and into every level of care in the practice.

Bringing Emotional Intelligence to Patient Communication Preferences

When communicating, you know your patients best. Remember too, that your website and portal can be your best friends. Posting as much information for families to independently resource from their homes will offer them the information they need and trust that you have their best care in mind. Pre- and post-procedure instructions are a great example of this. Consider these as conversations between staff and providers and patients a possible source of reassurance and TLC. If you are not sure which FAQs and other resource information are most pertinent, just ask your front desk and nurses—they will tell you!

A physician shared with me that as a medical school cohort, the students were trained beautifully on how to report data and test results, but they were not really trained on how to tell someone they have lost a loved one. You may possibly consider a meeting with providers to discuss how to relay such information to family members if needed. To get started, create empathetic prepared statements that providers can then make their own to remain consistent between providers and across patient communications.

Getting Back to ... Normal?

In times of stress, it's always good to try to maintain as much normalcy and routine as we can. Completely returning may take some time. Making sure everyone is aware of the potentially long timeframe allows the practice to work together as a whole while being mindful of everyone's stress. Keeping an eye on the goal to return to 100 percent restoration without pushing too hard toward or making it feel impossible is tricky, but being mindful can make all the difference for everyone.

That being said, you also have a business to run, and, as a leader, it is your job to keep it going in the most balanced way possible. This is where the emotional intelligence kicks in. And remember, you are not alone! You can surround yourself with an entire wonderful team that can collectively (with your guidance!) arrive at solutions that allows everyone to feel they are moving forward and on the path to returning to their normal lives.

Find a way to give thanks to everyone—pizza parties, gift certificates, bonuses, whatever seems most impactful, maybe even all the above!

6

Emotional Intelligence—Financial and Revenue Cycle Management

No one knows your practice and population better than you. As the practice director, your standards of behavior are displayed and relayed with every interaction, communication, and exchange of information that you go through with staff, providers and patients. Each day includes immediate, cognitive, process-oriented decision-making that directly affects the practice's revenue cycle. Utilizing emotional intelligence will help you understand, assess, and maintain a rapport and rhythm with patient collections that reflects confidence, accountability, and growth.

We all get caught up in rationalizations and emotions ... and can miss the common sense general big picture info.

Let's look at how emotional intelligence can help you with every facet and approach in your revenue cycle.

As you may remember, emotional intelligence is made up of two primary competencies: personal competence and social competence.

So there are personal competence and social competence, as well as the four categories and core skills of awareness and management that are essential to who you are. It is the part of us that is like no one else. I am what I am what I am. For example, I'm a little stubborn and will always stand up for the little guy. That will never change. It is in my demeanor ... (See what I mean?)

We all own distinguishing characteristics that make up our *persona*. How we act individually, interact, and react within human relationships is what makes us emotionally aware. It is how we are able to manage our behavior and, hopefully, present a very positive manner. This conscious perception adds to your critical thinking skills that helps you be more emotionally intelligent with your patients, staff and physicians.

One example of self-management skills with revenue cycle is how you will be communicating with and reacting to patients that are unhappy. An example could be a post-visit balance when a patient believed something was covered. Reflecting empathy and understanding of that patient's angst is essential to gain trust and feel comfortable in establishing a payment plan. We never want to place a patient in a place of shame in any situation, including financial.

Emotional intelligence also helps us control the impulses and how we maintain self-will, especially when a patient becomes irate. Calming a patient is a prime sampling of where we can focus on the continuing goal of compassionate care while acknowledging emotional details.

Leadership in the Face of Financial Concerns

"Honest people don't hide their deeds."

Emily Brontë, Wuthering Heights

Leadership includes financial responsibility for the practice's checks and balances. Including yours. Roughly 10 percent of the nation's healthcare revenue is lost through fraud. We are not exempt from these incidences, and they are increasing at an alarming rate. It is estimated that during a five-year period, over 80 percent of medical practices will experience embezzlement in one form or another. And of those committing the embezzlement, it is estimated that 70 percent have done this before with a previous medical practice.

Even with great policies and processes in place, we all tend to relax, especially when we have been working with the same people for a long time. We trust them, which is a natural progression in building human relationships. What we forget is that no one's life is static. As our lives change, so do our needs! Pay attention to what is going on in the lives of staff members. You can use your emotional intelligence to build trust but always keep that trust tempered with an awareness of the realities that require carefully monitored systems. The biggest factor leading to embezzlement is opportunity. The second factor other than opportunity? The loyalty factor! Never discount that most invaluable asset! Theft can increase or decrease depending upon the employee's personal loyalty to the manager, physician, practice, and patients.

Insurance Representative Relationships

Your payer accounts receivable is the principal portion of your income. Similar to politicians, it is always good, and professional, to have a good rapport with your payer representatives. While it can be beyond challenging at times to contact representatives on a personal level, access can usually be gained with persistence. There will be some point where you can establish some kind of connection and build the sort of professional rapport that helps everyone.

Attend insurance "fairs" and professional gatherings and seek out your local representatives to possibly have a fifteen-minute practice-specific conversation. Try to be in touch to make an appointment beforehand if possible. If new, find the time to introduce yourself and to get to know them. And let them get to know you. Your goal is to have a relationship where they remember a face and not a file.

Timing is everything! It is imperative that you be aware of contractual renewal and notification dates for maximum positioning for the most income potential as you negotiate a new agreement. The professional relationships you establish also include many people that you will form long-term relationships with and find yourself tapping into as a professional resource over the years. This is a valued relationship.

I have been able to maintain a connection with some of these representatives even as we have both over time changed positions and roles. It is a win-win professional association.

Emotional Intelligence and Patient Collections

We often hear that you never know where someone is coming from. This can be very true when handling patient collections too! Utilizing emotional intelligence grants us the knowledge to find out.

It's our job to find a respectful and yet impactful way to approach patients when asking for payment. Socially, this is where you clarify and affirm other's emotions as you converse. Relationship management is exactly that—the ability to use awareness of your own and others' emotions to manage interactions successfully.

This includes letting go of anticipating of what you are going to say next and instead sitting back, watching, and listening before you react. While you are thinking of what you want to say, you are not listening to what they are really saying. And that is pivotal to be able to respond meaningfully to the words and emotions that are being conveyed.

Your emotional intelligence quotient will grow as you practice reading between the lines and identifying the sensitivities involved in any situation you are in. We are animals with basic instincts. We become in tune with where we spend a lot of time. By spending a lot of time approaching interactions in this way, though it may be hard at first, you will learn to be better and better at it and be able to use that as a more and more effective tool. It is that simple because it is a progressive and natural reaction.

An unconventional but true example is from my waiting on tables through college. I could tell who the good tippers would be as soon as they entered the restaurant doors. I have no idea how. This was not something I tried to cultivate. It just happened. (By the way, this gift worked *very well* for me). There is no way I could do that today.

This is true with patient accounts receivable policies too. There are several ways you can improve your emotional intelligence when working with the revenue cycle. Know your patients and their needs, then utilize that awareness to improve collections in a productive and respectful manner.

Ponder these points and tangents of approach:

- Address a patient's stress points in a productive manner. For instance, arranging monthly payment dates around what is most convenient for the patient not the practice. Work with *their* pay schedule.

- Being aware of the patient's (and your) body language and other nonverbal communications.

- Choose your words wisely. Don't rush it.

- Approach and resolve a bad debt discussion in a constructive manner with a realistic and as positive as possible solution.

Patient Vulnerability

The process of collecting a debt successfully involves maneuvering through the emotions of the patient to a payment plan that can work for both you and the patient.

A patient feels incredibly vulnerable as they enter a room to establish a payment agreement. Remember, unless they've done this with you before, they have no idea what to expect, including what healthcare really costs. Our job is to create the easiest and most comfortable setting for every part of the patient experience, including what their financial obligations are according to their plan. Think about the questions you ask a patient as you set up an agreement. Keep in mind that patients are more apt to meet the agreement if you help them be part of the process, beginning with the date that payments are to be drawn to help them, and actually envision the payment.

Emotional Intelligence Impacts Your Bottom Line!

Researchers from Harvard Business School, Illinois State University, and the University of Bonn and the WHU - Otto Beisheim School of Management in Germany have all done really interesting work showing that it isn't just your intelligence scored by IQ measurements that determine your income levels, but that your emotional intelligence as scored by emotional quotient (EQ) measurements make the biggest difference.

> Research at the Harvard Business School has shown that emotional intelligence (EQ)—the ability to manage our own emotions and connect to the emotions of others—counts for twice as much as IQ and technical skills combined in determining who will be successful in their career and in life.

> Show me the money! Researchers from the University of Bonn in Germany, Illinois State University and Otto Beisheim School of Management in Germany, found that when individuals displayed emotional intelligence—the ability to perceive other people's emotions—they were more likely to bring home a bigger paycheck than their emotionally unaware colleagues.

Further research at Harvard University, the University of California-Riverside, and the University of Toronto found that surgeons who are high in communication skills like empathy, get sued less often. This makes sense, doesn't it?[15]

Wake up! Emotional intelligence can in fact be awakened and further developed in each of us. Awareness and emotional intelligence are relayed with every communication, interaction, and exchange with staff, providers, and patients. Gained knowledge blended with emotional intelligence can help design creative and compassionate methods that accelerate your patient and payer collections.

Emotional intelligence can invigorate both staff and patient engagement with financial responsibility.

This is an individual, as well as team-based, approach where most current patient collection strategies and approaches can easily be built into your collections processes so that they are personalized, fair to the patient, and improve your revenue cycle management processes.

Consequences that Can Affect Collections

Don't let *your* emotions get in the way of your abilities! Just when I'm telling you to make sure to engage in the patient's emotional responses, I'm going to offer a caveat. There are times when collectors can actually identify (too much) with a patient.

Let us set a scenario for an internal collection call to a patient. Think of the very possible setting where you are meeting with a patient with an older balance due from an insurance denial saying that it is non-covered, even though the insurance company had said at one point that it would be covered.

Sometimes a collector can tend to *over* identify with the patient who appears to be helpless. The collector then becomes overly empathetic. That can blur the psychological boundaries and result in identifying with the patient as a victim. They then may be a little more forgiving regarding an already overdue balance. Emotional self-management skills need to calm this sort of over-identification distress or the situation can lead to a more lenient negotiation that is less optimal for your practice. Don't take on their emotional state. Be aware of it.

If the collector is angry for whatever reason, but especially if they do not have a good relationship with the patient, a lack of self-control will also blur the lines and may actually lead to arguing with a patient. At that point, the fate of payment is decided, as the negotiation becomes a shouting match that ruins any possibility of collecting from the patient.

With internal collections, please be sure to keep current with local, state, and federal laws of what can and cannot be said. Check also with your collection agency, as they should be aware of appropriate verbiage and protocols when collecting from patients. This also allows you and your collection agency to work together. Apply these points where emotional intelligence can account greatly for your work success as you hire collections staff. Poor collectors tend to collect an average of 80 percent of their goal, while great collectors average 163 percent of their goals. Which employee would you like to have?

Introducing New Credit Card Policies to Patients

As with any new financial policy, introduce new credit card policies with careful planning. The timing of the introduction and who makes that introduction are critical details. It also helps greatly when you have already established an initial trust, which will make patients be more receptive to changes.

Although many see the front desk as the zone to add new tasks, this is best announced in the most patient receptive ways as possible. To be delivered with respect and effectively, it is much better received in a venue where they may absorb and consider the information. If they are learning about it for the first time as they are trying to engage credit card processing at the front desk, this change will feel forced upon them under pressure of time and location.

Some practices roll out new credit card policies with all patients, some choose to just initiate them with new. Some practices take a more plan-specific approach, and some first apply it to older or post-visit balances. In fact, you probably already know the patients you may first introduce this to as you read this paragraph.

The billing department could begin with accounts about to go to collections. You can also start with procedural, surgeries, treatments, or other larger amounts that could be broken out into a more affordable and predictable payments. Remember, you will only get one chance to truly introduce a new policy. First impressions are crucial as you strive to establish a fair agreement with the patient.

You know your patients best. Step-by-step planning includes clear, designated resources and assistance to carry it through successfully the first time in a personable and professional manner.

Interdepartmental (and Your) Support

Receptionists can feel like they are hamsters in a wheel. They just keep going and going and don't really feel the progress or results of their hard work. Angela, a receptionist dynamo, once expressed to me that she did not feel completion with her job. We all have to feel success with our work. It is affirmation of our value in the workplace.

Managers and clinical staff are able to approach a good deal of their work on a daily or a project base with an identifiable beginning, middle, and end where achievements can be completed and felt. To fully portray the value the front desk staff has, I reminded her that correctly entered demographic information is crucial to getting the claim paid the first time! Which impacts the entire revenue cycle positively.

The front desk also helps determine and set the pace of the patient flow, as appointments are set correctly and according to the reason for their visit. When a patient is in the exam room waiting to see the doctor on time, even with processing new patient information, she has done her job! When there is a crisis, the front desk staff are the ones usually contacting patients. And have I mentioned that they get to ask for money from sick people? So, you can see how we have to keep affirming the medical receptionist's role. Your patient's visit literally begins and ends with these staff members. Angela's question was a perfect example of someone looking for affirmation. And I was more than happy to do that for her.

For other staff members to get a feel and an appreciation about what it is like to be in other positions within the practice, roleplay with it in meetings. Present a challenging situation, switch roles, and have fun. Swap a nurse to follow the process of a front desk check in (e.g. why the paperwork at the front takes *soooooo* long!). Present the most bizarre and/or complicated situations for co-workers to deal with, sit back, and watch. Really, have fun with it. It's always good to have a laugh, with it being most especially helpful and bonding when we can laugh at ourselves a little bit and release a little tension together. And your staff will *really* appreciate your emphasizing their value in front of their colleagues!

"Happiness is an attitude. We either make ourselves miserable, or happy and strong. The amount of work is the same."

Francesca Reigler

Leadership Support in Customer Service

Leaders always set the example and every initiative begins with you.

Customer service is not about an employee spouting policies or simply saying what the patient wants to hear. It is truly serving the patient, anticipating their needs, and completing their sentences for them in a venue that can be fearful for some. We carry on the practice/patient mission together as leaders, constantly supporting our staff physicians in that effort.

Those in charge set the standards—every day. The very best customer service and patient-centered plans are not serviceable without management support and employees who are fully trained, comfortable, and confident when speaking with patients. Our emotional intelligence declares that customer relations management should always be approached in the most positive way. I have learned that this takes concerted and continued efforts to make this happen. Looking at the ROI of providing stellar service, or not, will confirm that it most often pays off, even with financial investments required to implement it.

Tip: Long-term employees help retain long-term patients. Patients value a predictable encounter, especially in a fearful setting. It offers a sense of security and familial feel when a patient recognizes staff members throughout the practice. This reassurance of "personal" care can also make it easier for us to collect payments, increase compliance, and improve outcomes!

Leading and Supporting Your Staff with Difficult Patients

Know Your Patient, Know Yourself

No one knows your practice better than you! It is worth repeating. To yourself. Out loud. A leader's role is priceless. We are the central resource and the *go-to* person for every single person in the practice. The first thing to recognize is a gained knowledge of your patient base along with an empathy that will help you deal better with difficult patients every single time.

At times, without even begin aware of it, we can have internal biases that prevent us from seeing the reality before us. We often do not notice gradual changes. To gain a greater understanding, it can be valuable to run demographic reports and see exactly how your populations have changed in the recent years.

Openly discussing these topics in staff meetings with respect and always in the light of improving patient care grants transparency and possible additional insight as to people's differences. Knowing your patient population will help you and your staff with addressing language barriers, cultural issues, and preferences.

One example is a typical financial issue, in some households, only one person handles all the bills, so a family member may not be prepared to remit their co-pay at check in and will wait for a bill. This patient may be unaware of other agreeable options, such as credit card on hold, and how we can honor a family's preferences with no pressure and a predictable guarantee of payment. This is a perfect example of where we can successfully resolve a possibly very difficult issue beforehand with respect and fairness to all parties.

Story

A Physician's Emotional Intelligence

I have the honor of working with an incredible practice in Connecticut. While I was working with the receptionists, a patient who had been seen that morning returned with a friend. A very angry friend. The patient was very pleasant while the friend had another goal in mind. This person stomped up to the front desk, screaming and yelling about a prescription that was not yet ready at the pharmacy. It was apparent that she had no intention of listening to anything and just wanted to scream.

The very experienced and well-spoken front desk person tried to calm her down in the most professional manner. By this time, the disrupter was so loud the physician had actually heard everything and came to the front desk.

He was so calm and reassuring in his approach. He very calmly invited the patient and friend to his office to discuss privately. They were in there for about five minutes. Afterwards he gently escorted them to the door, thanking them for coming by.

When the physician and I were meeting at the end of the day I asked him if he did not mind telling me what he had said that calmed things down so much. He said, "I was very confident in my care and know that I had addressed all her problems and concerns and wanted to reassure her of my compassion for my patients."

"If you continually place limits on everything you do, physical or anything else, it eventually spreads into your work and your personal life. There are no limits. There are only plateaus, and you must not stay there, you must go beyond them."

Bruce Lee

His self-confidence and awareness of his own actions enabled him to handle what otherwise may have been a very difficult situation in the most calming and positive way. A beautiful example of successful self-awareness and relationship management skills actually improving the quality of a relationship.

Consider the (Real) Source

When there is an issue with a patient and payment, begin with considering if the issue is a result of the patient or if it truly something arising from the practice's deficiencies or experience in handling this kind of concern. You can frequently alleviate a patient's bad mood or unsettling behavior by determining the underlying and *true* cause(s) of the problem.

Of course, it can seem hard not to take it personally when someone is screaming in your face, but, really, it's not. It is usually about the practice, and/or something else entirely that happened with them yesterday for example. It's just that we happen to be standing there while they are that upset! It can be tough avoiding being too defensive and unwind enough to know the appropriate words to say at the right time as well as when a compromise may be needed for a positive resolution.

When faced with these situations, you are hopefully engaging your emotional intelligence muscle. With every patient, the message leads directly to how the patient feels and reacts to that interaction. What impressions do we prefer?

Story

What Is the Real Reason?

While I was running a family practice with an urgent care, there was an established patient that noticed another patient going in before her even though she had been there for about thirty minutes. This patient was an established patient for at least ten years and her demeanor was typically friendly and quiet. That day, she was quite irate and asked to speak with a manager. A receptionist escorted her until we met in the hallway, and we walked together to my office.

At first, she was telling me how sick she was and had been waiting "way too long." After listening to her speak, and my confirming her concern a little longer, she relaxed. It turned out that she was far more concerned with being absent from her job and the fear of losing that job than how sick she was. So, the time factor was still big—but for a different reason. With her permission, we immediately contacted her employer explaining that she was held up and would be back at work as soon as possible. No HIPAA violations—just confirmed that the patient had approved us calling, with proper documentation of course!

All I did was listen to her, affirming her value, and addressing her needs as a patient. I was a manager that paid attention. It is also important to note that we had already established a trusting relationship. Remember, I mentioned that she was a long-standing patient and had a positive rapport. That of course carried over and made it easier for her to trust that we would care for her, as we always had in the past.

Imagine if she had been unhappy with our care leading up to that specific time and conversation, how that may have carried over. We are truly planting seeds with every conversation we have.

As mentioned before, role-playing is a great way to resolve and offer a positive message and real-life lesson related to difficult patients—particularly at staff meetings using actual situations that may have happened that very day. You will want to provide impact and particular value with any message that you deliver to your staff. People tend to remember situations when they become personalized. Stories that surprise are more likely to be shared. Make it personal.

You can then identify communicative difficulties and formulate how these incidents can be remedied. It is always beneficial to quickly debrief and weigh in on how the situation could have been handled better. There are always one or two items that you will be able to handle better or quicker the next time!

Also, grab that beautiful opportunity to publicly recognize an employee that has handled a situation impeccably well and with compassion as a great example. Good examples also serve as great training tools.

It is always encouraging to share positive experiences. Reinforcement of a successful exchange is a great way to avoid difficult conditions.

Meeting with the Patient: An Opportunity

When meeting with a patient, set the stage to establish the boundaries that you prefer. Choose a small, private, personable room that does not intimidate but welcomes a patient with soft light colors such as a light coffee or light green. Place a small desk or table, comfortable chairs, and a live plant if possible. This space is designed for you and the patient to arrive at a mutual and trusted agreement.

First, find the calm in yourself, then be objective and be honest with them. Expressing sincere empathy and giving your undivided attention and time can make a big difference in their attitude and softening those unkind behaviors.

Try taking a few deep breaths, allowing information to go through your emotional part of your brain to the common sense resolution part that will help you answer and respond in an appropriate manner. If needed, there is the option to leave the room for a moment to create some space.

Keep in mind that you can apologize without admitting culpability. Even if you are not the one who is at fault, it's okay to earnestly say, "We deeply regret this happened."

Use polite and firm language. If a patient begins a downward spiral of hostile language, do not allow yourself to lower to their level.

Say That Again?

Sometimes people repeat themselves because they feel like they're not being heard. You will quickly notice that patients will not hear a thing you have to say until they have said everything; they would like to go first. *Always* let them speak first.

Acknowledge their situation. A first response from you should always be "thank you," as it reflects your affirming their version as expressed to you. As you confirm and document their statement, clarify your interpretation by use the phrase, "Just to clarify, you have already … (e.g.) requested your prescription and are waiting at the pharmacy, correct?"

These answers are helpful because they define a possibly vague statement and will be seen as productive and working towards a solution.

The patient being part of the resolution and follow through also paves the way to smoother conversations.

Need Help?

If a patient is truly emotionally distraught, console them and give them the time and space they need. You may need a provider if the situation warrants it.

Guide them and insert phrases to help the complete the discussion so you may come up with a solution. A few key phrases that work well are: "How can I help you?", or "I'm trying to help you."

Sometimes, it is easier just to state the tension and get it out of the way and start again. "I feel like we are getting off on the wrong foot."

Postural Feedback!

This is the best two-minute exercise you can do for your confidence.

Confidence is a wonderful thing! One action we can take to experience a true confidence surge is "postural feedback." This only takes two minutes to do and awards instant results. This pose can be extremely helpful with situations such as dealing with a difficult patient, provider issue, or if you need to speak with a staff member.

Postural feedback leads to a greater feeling of confidence. The most well-known pose? Picture a superhero and you've got it! Stand up straight, hands on hips, chin up, chest out, and shoulders back. This also works great with family too by the way!

There are other poses such as spreading arms across the seat behind you or leaning over a table with your arms spread across the width of the table. The image is one that literally expands your physical presence.

Adding a meditation or breathing exercise to this pose can add to the overall impact and confidence.

Now consider points in your day and your lifetime when you can best engage this pose. Whether you're asking for a raise, approaching an employee or difficult patient or even a peer, this pose help you gain the confidence when you most need it.

A little over 100 seconds can really change your day!

Avoid a Defensive Posture

If you need to leave the room to compose yourself, do it. And remember that it's not about you, it's about the patient.

You may also be frustrated, but do not let that be the catalyst for you to overreact.

Realign your body language. Take little breaths. If the patient is becoming demanding, and you need to maintain control, it would be time to check how you are coming across. When you do that, your body language realigns.

"Self-control is strength. You have to get to a point where your mood doesn't shift based upon the insignificant actions of someone else. Don't allow others to control the direction of your life. Don't allow your emotions to overpower your intelligence."

Morgan Freeman

How Should I Say That?
Utilizing Scripts

Utilizing scripts can really help with unified messaging, especially when introducing a new policy or program such as credit card on hold or other financial policies.

Begin with a template, which are widely available, and then make it your own to add sincerity. Especially with a new policy, please be sure that there are accessible documents for low-vision or non-sighted patients, as well as someone they can be referred to for further information if needed. This is how we look competent to our patients.

As we develop awareness, self-management allows us to offer the right approach with all information originating from a central point. The right language can be challenging for some, so it is worth considering possible pre-scripting to assist.

A script does not have to sound artificial; it should be full of content that allows the deliverers to individualize their responses. For instance, when a patient asks about a financial policy regarding a high deductible plan, the main point is to get across enough introductory information to be able to discuss a payment plan or to refer on and have them speak with someone further about their account.

The response could be something like, "For a patient with a high deductible plan, we are requesting that $150 be paid at the time of check in to cover the office visit, and the other services may then be determined by you and your physician at the time of the visit."

The vital point is to make sure that everyone is using the same wording and version.

With any new policy or change, you are the conductor of the practice orchestra. Consider how each of us may listen to or create a piece of music. While we all may like the song, each of us tends to look for different parts within it. It could be the vocals, guitar, drums, horns, or the entire symphony. We all hear different segments and come together to create a symphony. Managers tend to compose the whole symphony. That's what true teamwork is. When you can, positive phrases are built from positive words. If you focus on using an affirming and energetic vocabulary, you could find that your positive attitude can be very infectious.

7

Build A Culture of Superior Communication

"No matter what job you have in life, your success will be determined 5 percent by your academic credentials, 15 percent by your professional experiences, and 80 percent by your communication skills."

Dr. Daniel Milstein

Successful executives and leaders communicate clear-cut visions, establish boundaries, and build bridges. Managers are the first to say that one of the most important factors for a positive organizational culture is communication, followed by leadership and staff engagement.

Be the Part and Be in Charge!

It's okay to be in charge! Each word from a practice leader carries a lot of weight. Be cognizant that the team will hear your voice with more impact than any other voice in the room.

Make a concerted effort to show you would like to exchange information by asking open-ended questions in a non-threatening manner to keep team members sharing information freely. For example, when asking an employee about their tasks and timing, a closed-ended question might be: "Why does it take more than two hours to balance and post the daily deposit?" versus an open-ended inquiry such as, "Tell me about your process and timing for balancing and posting the daily deposit."

Another example dealing with personal dynamics could be a closed-ended question like, "Why don't you get along with Ashley?" Compare this to asking an open-ended inquiry, like, "Help me understand your relationship with Ashley."

"Help me understand" is a wonderful welcoming quote that my friend and co-worker Margaret introduced to me. It can be the beginning of a conversation that reflects no judgment and 100 percent total acceptance.

Facilitating Conversations— Where Would You Like the Conversation to End?

Accept that it is normal that everyone has their own particular style and way of communicating—when listening as well as relaying information. To be effective, a leader must identify how individuals best communicate overall. Some respond better to weekly one-on-one meetings; another may thrive with "as needed" conversations.

Be aware of expectations and circumstances influencing how well someone communicates. Habitual tendencies or fear of poor performance can impact or prevent effective communication. If you find yourself heading towards a negative conclusion about someone's ability, pause and ask yourself, what factors could be affecting their behavior? This is where your emotional intelligence kicks in for a productive solution!

How do you deliver open and accessible communication between staff members when everyone's face seems to be stuck to a device all day long?

A quick disclaimer. I am truly one of those that is addicted to my smart phone. When I lose track of it, I am just a little nervous until I find it. It also seems like my face is looking at one or more of my devices at any given time throughout the day. Does this sound familiar to anyone else? Nonetheless, as a leader, you need to be able to reach your staff and have impactful conversations. Smart phone in hand or not.

- Create opportunities for face-to-face encounters. You may also get a quicker response to a question if you just stop by someone's desk versus sending an email.

- Make it personal—go out to lunch with co-workers. I remember my first day at my first job after college. The entire department went out to lunch for introductions. Of course, that may not be an option for now, but it is most important to take the time to get to know someone. Just like any other relationship, if you are familiar with each other, you are more able to have a real conversation. You may find that you get twice as much twice as fast compared to an email or text. Remember that body language is over 50 percent of communication.

- Meetings? Unless you are on call, no phones! If needed, you can set it up so that everyone puts their devices in a basket upon entering the room. The basket is then placed out of sight. If a basket is not an option, then phones should be silenced and placed away from view.

- Use paper. What?! You heard me correctly. When taking a consensus, asking someone to document their thoughts, or request a signature, use paper and pen. People tend to reflect a little more. More on this later in the chapter.

Build Bridges of Communication and Establish Boundaries

As you consider avenues of communication, think about how to highlight your natural communication strengths.

Keep in mind the time these efforts will take as well. Technology offers collaboration tools that can help you accelerate how communications content is developed, distributed, and measured.

Determine your preferred direct channels for individual, practice, or system-wide employee communiques: traditional memo, email, internal texting, electronic medical records (EMR), HR, or another platform, etc.

For ease of crossover, use channels your staff members are already tapping into, which allows for a number of options ... professional sites, Twitter, employee roundtables, periodic CEO blog and/or podcast. Communicate with clear and convincing messages that each staff member can identify with and build shared bonds.

A great example of positive communications? A hospital system near Atlanta often features staff members who are highlighted by the leaders of this organization as a sign of appreciation. What a constructive and encouraging reinforcement! I would want to put my best efforts forth if I knew they appreciated me that much!

"In everyone's life, at some time, our inner fire goes out. It is then burst into flame by an encounter with another human being. We should all be thankful for those people who rekindle the inner spirit."

Albert Schweitzer

Conversations That Count!

Conversations and interactions that build familiarity also build relationships, credibility, and comfort. One CEO I know makes continued efforts to be in contact with each one of the almost 300 employees with birthday cards, positive statements, anecdotes sent out with payroll, memos, emails, and other practice correspondences. Increase the value of your communications … the more people that know about some happening, it's only natural that they want to know about it more. This is networking!

Updates should feel like a personal connection and social media creates the impression of a relationship. Also, be aware of which media can be external as well as internal.

And don't forget to calculate the time needed to plan for communications development and delivery!

Trust is Vital!

We are more open and communicate more transparently if we trust in that relationship. Joel Peterson, the chairman of JetBlue has ten laws of trust.[16]

They include (*with my response following in italics.*):

Law One: Start with personal integrity. *What a great place to begin... hopefully inspiring a pride that comes with the integrity.*

Law Two: Invest in respect. *Respect is not automatic. It is earned and worth investing in. You can earn that respect one-on-one or as a group. Think of instances with other people that has helped you gain respect for them.*

Law Three: Empower others. *You have hopefully hired professionals. Let go and let them do their jobs. No need to micromanage.*

Law Four: Measure what you want to achieve. *I think benchmarking and positive outcomes says it all.*

Law Five: Create a common dream. *It can be the practice mission, project oriented, or a team statement.*

Law Six: Keep everyone informed. *Transparency initiates trust. You don't have to give all the information, but enough so everyone can do their jobs feeling valued and confident.*

Law Seven: Embrace respectful conflict. *We can still like each other and not agree on topics. These great banters can lead to excellent answers that work for most people. The best leaders hold back and listen as much as they speak up. Think like a mediator with no judging and come to the best solution possible for everyone.*

Law Eight: Show humility. *Yes*

Law Nine: Strive for win-win negotiations. *They call it an agreement for a reason. It should benefit both parties in an agreeable manner.*

Law Ten: Fix breaches immediately. *Take care of a problem as soon as it arises. Your staff is watching to see how you will handle issues and will respect you for handling it quickly.*

Story

Trust and Overseeing Roles

I once worked with a patient account services representative that performed all billing procedures for a family practice. She was phenomenal. She was excellent with the doctors, knew her coding, was great with patients, and the staff loved her.

At some point, projects and phone calls began to slip through the cracks and things were left unattended or not completed by month end. I asked her if everything was okay, and she said all was fine, no problems. Instead of looking further or really observing her role, I took her at her word, not realizing how much more she had gradually added to her workload without a complaint. Her performance continued to decrease, and patients were beginning to complain.

When you trust someone, you may take their word for it and not inquire any further. You may also want to leave an impression of trust in your staff members. But there are staff members who will continue to say yes and take on more work and more work, never requesting help even when they are obviously overloaded.

In retrospect, it was blatantly clear that I should have recognized at a much earlier point that we had been adding providers to her workload over the last two years. Even with the daily chaos, it is a manager's job to be in touch with and balance everyone's roles and capabilities. While I believed and depended upon her to tell me if there was an issue or if she needed help, I should have been more in tune with the flow, and her added workload, predicting and anticipating any issues before they developed into full-on problems.

Fortunately, we were able to have many meetings and resolved several issues, including providing her with additional assistance. While we were able to address this directly, some time had passed from when her workload had become unmanageable. I'm sure there were some incidences that may have easily been avoided had I done a better job of overseeing this person's work. There is nothing like real life to learn as we go. (Our emotional intelligence can catch this!)

In all, there is no better statement I can think of relating to emotional intelligence than Maya Angelou's observation, "I've learned that people will forget what you said, people will forget what you did, but people will never forget how you made them feel."

Communication— Beginning and Now

We are first taught how to communicate from our families, then school and other social activities. There are certain basic learnable skills that really can help you in life, including manners and how to be heard while being respectful and aware of others around you. I once had a boss who had been sent to "charm school" by our company. He was very proud of it because he felt much more capable to do his job in a comfortable pleasant way as he conversed with co-workers, etc.

It is always a plus when someone communicates well during the interview process. And that can be just the beginning.

> TalentSmart tested EQ alongside 33 other important workplace skills and found that EQ is the strongest predictor of performance, explaining a full 58 percent of success in all types of jobs….

> Of all the people we've studied at work, we've found that 90 percent of top performers are also high in EQ. On the flip side, just 20 percent of bottom performers are high in EQ. You can be a top performer without EQ, but the chances are slim.

Naturally, people with a high degree of EQ make more money, an average of $29,000 more per year than people with a low degree of emotional intelligence. The link between EQ and earnings is so direct that every point increase in EQ adds $1,300 to an annual salary.[17]

Increasing your EQ won't just pad your bank account, it'll make you happier and less stressed as well!

Your staff having strong emotional intelligence abilities is essential to offer the compassion to anticipate, recognize, and address patient's necessities. You will want to emanate empathy and have clarity and composure in possible stressful and difficult situations with practice issues as well.

Offices cultures range from serene to chaotic, but things can change in a second. Sound judgment is needed to maintain a respectful and courteous approach when balancing possible emergent and highly emotional situations.

Walls, Machines, and Situations = Barriers to Communication

"As human beings, our job in life is to help people realize how rare and valuable each one of us really is, that each of us has something that no one else has—or ever will have—something inside that is unique to all time. It's our job to encourage each other to discover that uniqueness and to provide ways of developing its expression."

Fred Rogers

Physical Barriers

There are barriers everywhere—verbal, visible, and situational. The simple presence of physical walls will literally limit your communication. A common example of managing barriers is addressing a physician's preference to have their own area with their nurse so they can carry out patient care most efficiently in their own way. That makes sense.

Unfortunately, what can happen is that teams then tend to work independently versus as a practice. Being sure to communicate the same message to everyone is instrumental in carrying out practice mission and goals. It never hurts to be reminded how wonderful everyone is in taking care of patients and this is how we like to do it.

A simple message and reminder can help standardize policies in an overall and affirming manner. This is where standing meetings and periodic events help bring everybody together while respecting everyone's autonomy in the practice.

Technology Barriers

Practice technology—such a love/hate relationship! At times it can be so frustrating or feel inadequate or severely outdated. Keep an eye out for when your staff gets to a point where they are constantly working around a program or a machine. Make sure it is addressed as soon as possible.

As you remedy issues with their day-to-day technology needs, you will also notice the morale and efficiency improve as your staff will be grateful for tools that work!

If purchasing new technology or equipment seems to be cost prohibitive, run a quick and dirty pro forma to forecast your income and expenditures, including what your cost for labor will be with existing technology versus an update or newer technologies. This will help with physician buy-in, as the document will show clear financial advantage.

Consider also the fact that you will eventually have to invest and update systems. Why not have it work for you and your practice as soon as it can, saving labor (which is most typically your highest expense)? Just as physicians need their instruments to work precisely, your staff should be reassured that their equipment and systems will work just as well, allowing them to better care for patients.

Situational Barriers

There are also situational barriers. These barriers are ones you may often forgo if you don't take the time to observe and think about it. The best leaders are mindful of employee morale and performance, cognizant of operations, and in touch with physicians on a steady basis. These actions alone will help you greatly in reducing those barriers. The "in between the lines" knowledge you have gained affords an overall perception that no one else has. Use that in the most positive way.

Cultural Differences

Mannerisms, customs, phrases that may or may not be used in general social protocols can place barriers between people trying to have a conversation or interaction. Sometimes it can be inflection of the voice or the way someone stands that can be interpreted incorrectly and misunderstood. This is also true of simply being in a different department or location with an entirely different environment. Build bridges that will naturally occur during face-to-face meetings as well as general events so all staff hear the same message.

Nonverbal Clues

Paying attention to body language and facial expression can tell you a lot. This is where the eye to eye contact and face-to-face meetings can expressly make a difference with our communication, especially when in a challenging situation. Is the person that you are meeting pensive with their arms and legs twisted like a pretzel? Or relaxed and freely offering information?

Micromanaging

Staff engagement strategies can be undermined by a stifling approach and style. Micromanaging is a common behavior among those who lead in practices. As an administrator or physician, we want to know that things will be done in the way they should be. It's that simple sometimes. But micromanaging is exhausting for everyone involved. There needs to be a balance. It is easier for some of us to let go than others. You know who you are!

If you are someone that has trouble with this, be aware that your staff have already tuned you out after the twentieth time you asked if they have completed something yet. They do not hear you anymore. I once had the most amazing boss, and one of the smartest people on the planet. But the micromanagement made me leave. I am a professional and would like to be treated that way. My only thought was, "Please leave me alone and let me do my job."

Remember, you want your words to be heard with more force and to have what you say taken seriously. You can be in tune in a non-invasive way as you converse, confirm, and connect.

Distractions

Employees may want to get their job done but find it impossible to do so if they have to deal with interruptions such as staff, noise, and other duties. As administrators and physicians, we already know about the front desk and some nursing duties where it can be like Grand Central Station on any given day.

There is a pediatric practice I work with where the patient accounts manager's office was right near the patient lobby. Children were literally on the other side of the wall from her office bouncing balls against the wall. It was very hard for her to concentrate. This person would actually grow weary through the day trying to focus and get her job done. She now has a new office and a lot more energy to spend on her role.

It is not uncommon for us to be distracted and focus only on what we need to get done when delegating tasks or projects to staff. It's natural, as we may feel pressured or overwhelmed, and therefore do not take everything or everyone else into account.

For example, if we ask for a staff member's help, we may not be considering that they are also assisting filling in for someone else that week, and their day may already be a delicate balance. In addition, they may be afraid to speak up. Not a good formula for success, morale, or loyalty. It is your role to be mindful of such circumstances.

And then there are times (we've all had the experience) of starting one project and everything just seems to explode from that point on. A real Pandora's box. You start one part of it, and it turns out to be a million other things you have to do to make it happen. That is okay. Recognize it, strategize, and meet with key players to redefine your timeline and extra assistance if able.

If not, sectioning off the project may be a better option so you feel that success along the way and staff and patients continue to benefit from changes. Sometimes you can control things and sometimes you have to roll with the punches, doing what you can when you can.

Taking a Moment to Take a Moment

Taking a breath is important, especially when making fast decisions. Sometimes you will feel such an urgency to get something done and realize too late that you should have taken more time and completed the task much more carefully and thoroughly. This barrier can be quite costly and not caught until too late. It is also the hardest to catch because you are often in the middle of a crisis or emergency situation and you don't think you have the time to stop.

It is more than worth it to take five minutes with the right people in the room to review the situation before taking the next step and moving forward. Do you have someone who can look at your plan objectively? In meetings, be sure to take notes to capture what was actually said to avoid misinterpretations. Also cover what is typically done, especially smaller details that can really help and support larger tasks or more urgent matters. It is imperative to take a moment to assess fundamental and vital priorities as you determine what to do next.

Confabulation

I bring up this term because it proves the argument beyond a doubt for documenting discussions and policies as they occur. Clarity is needed when making plans and decisions. There should be a gathering of documented information rather than relying on someone recalling what someone else said. Not documenting thoroughly is a barrier that can keep you from moving forward.

Confabulation was identified and coined by Karl Bonhoeffer, Arnold Pick, and Carl Wernicke around 1900. This is a symptom of various memory disorders that can include made up stories where people literally fill in memory gaps with random items in their memory.

Our brains can and will make up information in the absence of actual understanding, effortlessly filling in for the missing information without any input from our conscious thoughts. When your brain is confabulating, you will not be aware of it as it occurs. Think about a memory you have from a long time ago where some of the details are not quite clear. As you tell someone about this, it is very easy to fill in with another memory or something you believe it might be or something simply pops up. You have to be very careful with this to ensure facts like dates and figures are not confused.

Complacency

Someone once said to me that when you become comfortable in your job, it's time to move on. While I am not sure if that is necessarily true, we definitely become relaxed in a position that we are used to. We also tend to go to our most comfortable spot and stay there as a protective measure. This conflicts directly with our role as catalyst, moving forward in the most progressive way for the practice and patients. Relaxing is not in our vocabulary. This is part of the conscious decision that we make as we continue to move forward professionally as well.

Overload

Becoming overloaded is an obstacle that is quite obvious and some of us know all too well! Each of us has our signs and cues as to when this occurs. We may be backed up on reviews or formatting schedules along with twenty other things! I can always tell when it hits me because I begin to lose things. (Sometimes I am a little too organized).

There is always something! If there weren't, we would not have a job. The difference is how much we can handle and our level of flexibility at any given moment. Physicians may be severely backed up with notes, approving refills, or reviewing results.

The key is being cognizant of these cues so that we can catch the overloading in time to balance our role, and maybe, others in their roles, accordingly. If delegation and other resources are not available, all we can do is prioritize. The other part of awareness with this quotient is to make your boss cognizant of it as you work through jobs and projects. We are only human and can only do so much.

Already Established Bias

Consider this: if I love my medical director, when they ask me to do something, I am there and ready to do it! If I don't like them, I still do it, but sometimes with resentment. Now that is a giant obstruction! That not only affects attitude and timing but potentially doing as thorough a job as possible. Many of us, of course, will give 150 percent no matter who is requesting. But think of how many other people's performances *could* be affected? We listen to and believe individuals that we trust more than ones we don't. It's that simple and direct. By the way, this is true for how our staff feels about us too!

Keep in Mind!

There will always be barriers. We are all different people with different hearts. Our hesitations are sometimes tied to fears from past experiences or are personal and go to our core. Emotions have a purpose. Leaders get to correlate and effectively collaborate everyone's angsts and confidences to gain the best and maximum potential from each employee and the practice.

Establish a Core Group that You Know Will Be Honest with You

Establishing a group of people who can be honest with you about challenges you face is key to being able to grow. The most optimum sampling would be a blend of people from personal and professional life. It will not take long to recognize patterns in their responses. I have always believed that when more than two people tell you the same thing in the same day, they are usually right! Let this candid honesty add strength to your work to grow confident decision-making and insight into successfully resolving issues.

The act of sharing and learning from others is every bit as important as what you learn. When you have this, trust is in easy reach. It becomes believable that you will be able to improve yourself and do things in the future that are currently beyond you. A very affirming and fulfilling goal!

Timing (and Approach) Are Everything!

Timing is everything when trying to communicate and be heard. While every office is different, there are some commonalities with scheduling accessibilities. Avoid Monday and Friday and never expect to get time with someone at the beginning or ending of any day, which leaves the early to middle of the day and week as when most people have available time in their schedules.

Be Respectful of the Impacts

Whatever message you are communicating will have some sort of impact. Try to be aware of what that will be, as being able to take that into account will enable you to show respect towards those receiving the message. Showing respect is an integral part of any interaction and introducing change can be a major disruptor to those who strongly agree with the current status quo. This is truly hard for some.

I have to carefully consider that I may be presenting something that can result in substantial impact to someone's daily life in an uncomfortable way.

This is actually a time to *remove* emotion and present as true a business observation as you can with a provided solution. Think of where you want the conversation to go so it may end on an onward positive note. How will it save time or make one's daily life better? Help them see beyond the change towards the benefit. It is easier for anyone to accept recommendations when the approach is authentic and genuine in intent.

Also, noting the way someone reacts when they don't get their way certainly shows their true colors. When a person shows you how they are the first time, please believe them.

Have you ever noticed when someone you really like has a really good day, it just adds to your admiration, but if you don't like them and they did something great, you think they just had a lucky day? It's that first impression along with other exchanges along the way that help us cement our opinion of someone. Once made, opinions can be very hard to change.

Be Aware of Others' Priorities

Keep in mind that everyone's priorities are different. Not everyone has the same gusto and dedication as the physicians and leaders of the practice. Everyone sees their value and contribution in their own way depending upon their role, length of time in that role, length of time in that position, and/or ownership of the practice. Some employees may not have the same dedication as a manager. You may know that, but it can be easy to forget. Some staff members are there for a job while others are wanting a more long-term career path and role in the practice that could possibly result in a leadership position.

Another example is someone who only needs to work part time. Is there a true 100 percent dedication? This is just an example. Let me say that I have had part time employees who were absolutely stellar and just as dedicated as full-time. We also may have great and devoted employees that draw the line at working overtime and extra Saturdays when they would rather be with their family. We all have our own lives that hopefully balance with our professional ones.

We never know … with any employee, someone's spouse may have a terminal illness, or they may have more than one job. Their family is always number one!

> *"Speak in such a way that others love to listen to you.*
> *Listen in such a way that others love to speak to you."*
>
> *Anonymous*

This is a perfect example of why it is imperative that we clearly communicate to each staff member exactly what their job is and how much more they may be asked to do, such as covering for other staff and working a few late nights when needed.

As an employer we need our staff to be flexible even as we support their work-life balance.

This is where mission statements, meetings, staff get-togethers, and any bonding experience you can promote with your staff will greatly help inspire and support a group vision.

Each Staff Member Has A Voice

One of the most common assertions staff members say is "We should all have a voice." This is usually brought up in staff meetings as I am discussing communication and they get a chance to speak up.

It only takes a few moments to listen to someone who knows that this is their only time to speak up. This is where staff engagement can begin!

Please let them talk! It begins with the person who is inquisitive and wants to know and do more than their job. As a staff member, engagement is something you can control, something you can activate with a little push. Make sure they feel they can ask you anything. You never know what they might bring to the table until you do! Do not pre-emptively squash any possible initiative.

With purpose, you're more likely to see your employees working with shared goals. This helps facilitate relationships and connections that contribute and lead to the practice's success!

As employers, we can help employees lean into what they are good at, and potentially focus on strengths they may have not even been aware of. Your job is to awaken the best capabilities for each employee's role and their part in the practice.

During conversations, ask them what their proudest accom plishments and greatest regrets are. Watch them brighten up as they help you understand their true demeanor and preferences. These conversations and interactions actively promote staff involvement.

Those who feel "listened to" have feelings of trust if your communications are strategically unified. True listening means focusing only on what the other person is saying. Again, it's about understanding their message, not what your anticipated response will be. Being able to set aside your communication goals and listen to what they are actually saying is so important. This is a most vital skill.

Don't Get Cocky!

Do not let your pride get in the way of your self-awareness and be ready to accept imperfections. It is okay to be a perfectly imperfect human. Being prideful may come from insecurity, and it often shows. Relax and let others see you as human—and own up to any mistakes when you make them. There are some people who find it easier to communicate with those who are humble.

Intelligence and listening are similar, as we each like to and tend to believe that we are above average. Travis Bradberry, Ph.D., a well-known author in the field of emotional intelligence, cited a study from Wright State University that was a broad cross-vertical survey of more than 8,000 people. Almost all survey participants believed they listened at least as well as, or better, than their co-workers. As he states, "We know intuitively that many of them are wrong."[18]

Clarify, Communicate, Confirm, and Connect!

The most important first step in communicating in a way that you can be heard is using positive body language. Being aware of your body language and tone and being as positive as you can will help things greatly. Offer comfortable seating. Take notes and lean forward as you are listening. And, yes lots of eye contact (worth repeating).

Body language is nonverbal communication. These are the observable factors that can impact how you feel about the entire conversation without you even realizing it. For example, do they look at you directly, smiling and ready to shake your hand? And how is someone seated in their chair? Do they look open or defensive? Are their arms and legs both crossed? Are they nervous about making eye contact? And how do you remain aware of all these hints that are being given? This alertness helps greatly, especially in an uncomfortable situation.

Eye contact is also vital whenever possible. This alone can help gain trust and show honesty and authenticity. As you are meeting with people, keep in mind these simple tips:

- Be seated in an open way with arms open.
- As you are listening, lean towards the person discussing to relay that you are a captive audience.
- Try to have the meeting location appropriate for the number of people. Two or three people do not need a massive conference table and something that large can be experienced as an intimidating and impersonal physical barrier.

Don't Pass Judgment

Being open minded is so important, but it can also be quite difficult. We have to eliminate already formed biases and tendencies that can sway us in many different directions. Be less guarded, remembering your position establishing what is most important to get the job done. There is no passing judgment, just understanding what everyone is saying. That is good communication!

Keep your mouth closed. Just that. Please listen.

Mirroring Body Language

When someone says, "Go to where they are," what does that mean? It means to enter their world, to perceive as they do. Connecting on yet another level makes people feel reassured and safe

One thing that we find that occurs very naturally, especially when engrossed in conversation, is that we tend to reflect each other's posture, tone, and even accent. I have found myself doing this most often, without even noticing it, while interviewing. We are animals and have our own instinctive movements without being aware of them at times.

This is typically done to please the person you are conversing with or when you feel a rapport. With work situations, this most often occurs during interviews, networking, peer conversations, and meetings. Everyone in the conversation will feel more connected if the participants are engaging in mirroring. It is unconsciously done, and it is also unconsciously received as a positive thing.

This mirroring can be very beneficial around the office as well as external business relationships such as negotiating a payer contract. In fact, in a 2008 study in the *Journal of Experimental Social Psychology*, "62 students were assigned to negotiate with other students. Those who mirrored others' posture and speech reached a settlement 67 percent of the time, while those who didn't reached a settlement only 12.5 percent of the time."[19]

It is not a far stretch for your staff to carry this into discussing an uncomfortable situation with a staff member or working with patients as you are establishing a payment agreement. Utilizing mirroring may make them feel a little more comfortable and trusting, which can result in making more successful agreements that will be honored. If they are trying to make eye contact and you meet them, that's an excellent start. Mirroring also includes verbal reflection. Some will repeat the last three or four words the other person spoke, inviting them to speak a little more and carry on a fruitful conversation.

Additionally, research has shown that shared behaviors can actually go beyond mimicking. As part of a study published in 2016, and co-written by Dr. Uri Hasson, an associate professor of psychology and neuroscience at Princeton University, functional MRIs were conducted, and it was found that those engaged in mutual mirroring are "dynamically coupled." The brains of both the person speaking and the person listening showed evidence that they reacted and adapted to signals from each other. Dr. Hasson likened the phenomena to wireless connectivity. "The brain's mirroring capacity is the basis for this interplay of signals and reactions, and nonverbal cues enhance it." [20]

In thinking about this in our daily lives, my husband and I will often notice that we are sitting in the same exact position. I take that as a good sign.

Mirroring body language can be incredibly helpful, but at the same time, you need to focus on being authentic and honest and not overdoing it. Don't go too far. We want it to be an unspoken and unnoticed not obvious behavior. Also, now that you are aware of it, be sure to avoid negative mirroring, where you amplify a person's negative body position or demeanor.

Consider different situations you may have throughout your day. Trying to get across to a difficult employee or a physician or patient can be challenging. If we can meet them in a way that is optimistic, respectful, and productive, hopefully that will lead towards a good result. I have some tips that employ emotional intelligence and being aware of your body's movements.

A previous connection will help things along before even walking into the room. If that is not already present, literally and physically stand with and in front of that person so there is an introduction to the "whole you" rather than just the half of you seen from behind the desk as you greet someone. A full and open introduction is the right starting point. Consider that first impression and interaction. Also, enter into the conversation knowing that listening to the other person and understanding their priorities is now *your* priority.

You can begin by simply tilting your head, showing focus on the conversation and nodding in agreement when you feel appropriate. Eye contact is always a plus, but not so much it makes the other person wonder why you're looking at them so much!

Approaching the other person's posture, tone, and other not-too-obvious behaviors would be the next step as you observe and take note of what else you may or may not need to do to accomplish your desired result. Matching the other person's pace in conversation is also a good grounding and trust-building technique.

Just as with other communications, avoid offering false compliments or mirroring negative nonverbal signs. Two examples of a negative nonverbal would be crossing your arms or backing away from someone.

If you're not comfortable with actively engaging in mirroring, do not worry about it, and let the connection occur naturally. The fact that you are considering mirroring during the conversation shows that you are also focused on listening and the other person's thoughts. That shows engagement and that you are sincere, which will show and benefit the conversation.

Look for more subtle nuances of behavior. Such as someone who may tap their fingers on a desk or rub their chin as they make a point. We often do these things without even being aware of them. Everyone has their "tell." Salespeople will tell you this is often the "clincher."

As you are able to engage mirroring in the most positive way, you will soon notice that it starts occurring without you even thinking about it. Be aware of yourself and others and allow your emotional intelligence to kick in. Pay attention to others' cues and observe what you are picking up as we tap into mirroring behaviors. Blending emotional intelligence, body language and mirroring can generate favorable interactions towards most constructive results.

"Silence is sometimes the best answer."

Tenzin Gyatso, The 14th Dalai Lama

Story

Stay in the Lines? Or Outside with Wild Abandon!?

There was a summer when one of my friends and I would endlessly draw and color in our coloring books. Her home had a massive breezeway between the house and garage, the perfect location to place restless children on a warm afternoon. I loved the plethora of colors in crayons, markers, pencils, as well as the array of coloring books to choose from. It was like a dream.

As I filled in the pictures, I was enjoying what the picture could be, not concerned with lines and boundaries. My friend was just the opposite, almost militant in her controlling every circle and edge until she completed coloring in each portion 100 percent filled in perfectly even tones. Very different approaches and yet, all goals were met.

"My way or the highway" equates to doors being slammed shut and causes two things: a decrease in productivity and an increase in ineffectual activity.

Sometimes it's best to approach from a totally different angle. Creative people do not like push-back and respond best as problem-solvers. If we are able to furnish the training and tools to add momentum to their efforts, the results will be worth it.

Use Paper, What?!

While we all have our own approaches, it is still beneficial to have some kind of established (and documented) launching point as we approach a problem that we would like to address and resolve within a short period of time.

Ironically, one idea has us returning to paper. There are still some very good arguments for this medium. I personally believe that if someone signs a document, they take it more seriously than signing on a screen. I also think that as we are mulling something over, sometimes it's good to enhance different senses as we work through an issue. For example, the smell and feel of the paper may provide a subliminal emotional reaction to our earliest school days and learning experiences. Our thought processes become more subjective.

One well-known format is the executive summary, which is a beautiful document. Consider a customized briefing document with the intent to launch the decision-making process towards a quick resolve. Geoffrey James, contributing editor at *Inc.com*, in his online article, "Adios, PowerPoint. This Simple Document Template Makes Meetings Shorter, Sweeter, and Smarter," outlines the following six-pointed plan to achieve this process:

1. *The Challenge.* This defines "where we are now" and is always either a problem or an opportunity.

2. *The Undesired Outcome.* This defines "where we don't want to be"—what will happen if the problem or opportunity is not addressed.

3. *The Desired Outcome.* This defines "where we do want to be," which should obviously be better than the undesired outcome.

4. *The Proposed Solution.* This defines what must be done to avoid the undesired outcome and achieve the desired one.

5. *The Risk Remover.* Why the proposed solution is likely to succeed and unlikely to fail.

6. *The Call to Action.* The decision you want made that will put the solution into motion to achieve the desired outcome. [21]

Some points that can help this along:

- ◆ Allow a specific amount of time for each person to document their thoughts.

- ◆ Each point is to be responded to with a sentence and short paragraph following.

- ◆ Let writing this by hand allow you to focus on this one issue without any beeps or alerts.

- ◆ Study how this format may be helpful for many different kinds of meetings.

From one on ones to a staff retreat, each person can enter with what they believe is the problem or the answer to the problem at each point. What a great way to get a snapshot consensus of what people believe and truly helps answer a problem! This format can also offer varied approaches dependent upon the level or specifics of a project to be addressed. A good option for anyone who wants to have a direct approach is a conversation. Some items can be addressed in a short and sweet manner, especially if we set it up that way!

Observations for Improving and Bonding (in Their Space)

In your ongoing efforts to identify barriers, you will need to engage with your staff "where they live." This sort of observational approach also helps troubleshoot operational issues you may not otherwise see unless you're actually in their area. Nothing gives a staff member more pride than showing you what they do.

Ask these three simple questions:

1. What do you like about your job?

2. What do you not like about your job?

3. How would you change your job?

It's like having a teenager behind the wheel of a car. They tend to tell you everything, and they love this sort of approach. I believe it is because they feel ownership of the space.

Give this time and do it thoroughly. Taking the time is an investment in each employee and potential for improving practice-wide policies. This is also a moment for them to shine and tell you exactly what they do, hopefully with a lot of pride. Staff members will relay a lot more respect when the boss shares their space and observes their exact role and contribution to the practice, affirming their value.

The employee "angsts" I hear about the most are the phone system, inter-office communications, being noticed, and of course the practice management (PM) and EMR systems. While this is of no surprise, I still listen to them and look at the little details that *they know* will make their job easier.

Use your listening skills and go deeper with each comment to identify what the most positive next step to resolve issues can be. That's what really helps; your staff will most appreciate those changes that help them every day.

If you are interested in more tracking and monitoring, there are also many healthcare-specific apps that are available (many for free!) that can measure and have the potential of increasing your staff's productivity numbers.

Use Real Life in Understanding Your Staff

People will open up and trust you *only* when they feel understood.

Story

How do you tell someone they smell?

I once had a staff member who was very friendly and personable. The interviewing went very well with excellent references.

After the first few days, we also noticed that she had a very strong body odor and the issue needed to be approached. Of course, I had no idea what to say, and I definitely did not want to hurt her feelings. She also appeared a little sensitive, and I wanted to be appropriate and be sure not to invade her privacy in case it may be result of an illness or other issue that was not my concern.

She entered my office smiling, took a seat, and we exchanged a few pleasantries. I told her that there were some concerns that as she came into work there was a very strong scent. I never said body odor. We did not know if it was coming from her clothing, her car, pets, or some other circumstance. I showed her where I kept a container of talcum powder for myself. I offered her one of her own and suggested that each day when she comes in to put some on and let's see what happens. Then I held my breath.

Needless to say, I felt much trepidation as I was suggesting this, not knowing what her reaction would be. She actually thanked me for telling her, and she respected me for approaching her about that. Her behavior continued to be loyal and hard-working, and she became unfailing in using talcum powder one or two times while she was working.

I am beyond thankful that she was approachable. Approaching a difficult issue with honestly and understanding is not easy. An authentic approach that relays acceptance, not punishment, typically leads to a positive mutual understanding.

8

Time Management, Operations, and How to Protect Your Calendar!

"Nothing will work unless you do."

Maya Angelou

Know Where You Stand and Be Realistic

One administrator I know spends about 80 percent of his time on human resources. He walks around the entire practice twice a day, once in the morning and once in the afternoon. Another manager says that they spend at least 20 percent of the day coaching and 25 percent on financial and contract issues. They also have a tiered huddle each day that begins with physicians and staff and daily happenings and concerns, then regionally, followed by a foundation huddle, and ending with hospital leaders. Leaders remain engaged as they each take turns being in charge of the daily huddles.

A manager's life is never boring! There are so many distractions. All you need is something shiny! Between personnel issues, provider requests, contracts, compliance, etc. I believe you can predict about two hours per day and the rest comes to you!

You spend a lot of your day putting out fires, which can cause difficulties in allowing time needed to focus on foundational projects and concerns.

A great first and beginning point of approach in managing your time is to block out as much as you can, as soon as you can, including vacation time, so you are more able to work around already built in commitments.

A time management pointer is to build in a safety buffer for deadlines. The date is set on your calendar as two weeks previous to the actual date. This allows for emergencies and other unforeseen circumstances to be front and center, if warranted, and still bring the project to completion on time.

Think of a jar of pebbles. You place the big ones first to make sure there is room and then place the smaller ones around it.

Look at all the papers on your desk. Yes, even that little pile that's been sitting there forever. The best news about those really old piles is that you can usually throw at least half of them away!

Move distractions and remain focused by placing only what you will be working on within arm's reach. Anything else is a potential diversion and moved to a different area. If you are clearing your desk and run across something that takes less than five minutes, go ahead and do it! That pile will be gone in no time!

To see the reverse side, some say it is actually healthy to have a messy desk, that it might even spark creativity and helps people see other sides to an approach or solution! Disorganization is not to be confused with cleanliness. It's just like a child's room; everything may be in piles, but they know exactly where each item needed is. But we still don't want old food containers in the mix!

A mistake is sometimes trying to contain creativity with physical barriers such as smaller, rigid, and cold workspaces. Offering a choice of smaller or larger rooms in deep blues and greens depending upon the need offers a break from conventional spaces.

Any new approach is a fresh way to arrive at a solution. Stepping outside the circle is hard sometimes but is very freeing.

Regarding your and other's organization, ask vendors, every single one, from payroll to PM/EMR systems, what they have to offer that can save you and your staff's time. Utilize all electronic avenues available, but do not discount paper when it can be more impactful.

These are big ticket items that most likely be utilized on a deeper level high most employees. You are already paying for them! Inquire about those big and little pebbles that can save you and your staff time.

"If you hear a voice within you say, 'You cannot paint,' then by all means paint, and that voice will be silenced."

Vincent Van Gogh

Clear Your Desk of Devices

Mobile devices are a blessing but also a curse—don't let yours control you! For a number of us, this can be literally excruciating. We check our mobile phones an average of 182 times a day. They are distracting even when we are not using it. That is equivalent to another person (or 50 of your best friends) in the room!

Simply having your phone in view, without touching it, has been shown to reduce performance in tests, according to a study from the University of Southern Maine. It was found that,

> Results of studies reported here provide further evidence that the 'mere presence' of a mobile phone may be sufficiently distracting to produce diminished attention and deficits in task-performance, especially for tasks with greater attentional and cognitive demands. The implications for such an unintended negative consequence may be quite wide-ranging (for example, productivity in school and the workplace).[22]

Place your device behind you. Trust me. If it needs you, it will let you know.

Meetings and timing are also so important to manage for your sake and others. The Babylonians created the concept we now call an "hour," which sounds like a nice round number, and many of our meetings are rounded out to that amount.

Many managers will tell you that they spend more time in meetings than performing their actual job. It can be a constant battle to keep up with the daily events and performing duties to their own personal satisfaction. A common concern is that their lack of presence in the practice's daily flow observing and among staff would begin to be reflected in morale. This can be a quick turnaround in a downward spiral affecting the entire practice's balance and culture.

Consider Parkinson's law, that says, "Work expands to fill the time available for its completion." So, naturally, if we assign a certain amount of time for a meeting, we tend to fill it. However, that may not be needed. For your calendar, try shorter meetings. One on ones especially do not need to be longer than 30 minutes and huddles should be no longer than 10 or 15 minutes.

Start with a universal time shorter than one hour and vary from there depending upon topic. The group can take it from there. Even shaving 10 minutes off a meeting leaves ample time to get quite a few things done. We work with physicians all the time to trim seconds off each visit to save them time. Now we can do the same for us as well as our staff. We can accomplish even more in the same amount of time!

What Is Your Office Footprint?

We have all had to be creative with the space we have. What were once large closets have been known to have been turned into compact offices. While respecting patient and other income generating areas, we also must be aware of how this affects the practice's everyday work/patient flow and satisfaction.

For example, how can patients that need to speak with a billing department before being seen get back on time if the billing office is across the building and three staircases away?

Also consider, does the front desk offer the appropriate amount of space or is it like a cockpit? Is the lab the size of a postage stamp?

We tend to make do with what we have, which is great and a conserving style. But be careful to not let gradual changes in furniture or working spaces become a permanent negative dynamic that forces your best staff to look elsewhere for a position with more open and pleasant working areas. It is instinctual. We are animals and need our own space.

"Let your life go from black and white to technicolor."

Daymond John

Email

Email is the gift that keeps on giving—and giving! Just like voice-mails, you can make this a predictable flow by having a monitor just for email. As you review emails, one of these actions will apply: delete, delegate, respond, defer, and do.

Respond quickly to avoid follow up inquiries, and yet another email.

When writing an email, every word matters. Save time and add clarity with straightforward and concise messages.

Use bullets if you think that will help clarify timing for example, or specific points you would like to emphasize. Sometimes in healthcare, we need a glossary for all of the acronyms and terms.

Just like your desk, clean out your inbox constantly. Utilize flags for color coding and quick identity.

No never-ending chain emails please! The last thing we need to add to our workload is sorting through the 30 responses to an email that may only involve a few of the people included. Sometimes it is easier to simplify and stick your head around the corner for a conversation instead. One important factor is that you cannot tell someone's attitude from an email. Sometimes face-to-face remains the best approach.

"Live as if you were to die tomorrow. Learn as if you were to live forever."

Mahatma Gandhi

Delegation

Who knew our time would ever be seen at such a premium? In terms of forecasting revenue, administrators can easily be viewed as "income generating space" and their time should be planned and rationed as such. It is that valuable.

So, where would you like your time spent? What is your return on investment for the practice?

At times, one of the best options is to delegate. In fact, as we grow in our jobs and want others to grow in theirs, it is more than appropriate to pass on duties. When I was a manager, there was a staff member who wanted to move up, and I needed help with accounts payable. I delegated part of the process, saving me a lot of time, and she got to become more involved with the practice. This is a great example of how carefully delegating also can help the practice grow as a whole. As you determine what to delegate and to whom, think about the "rights" of delegation: right task, who, circumstances, person, direction or communication, and right supervision/feedback.

It is also good to include other key staff in the delegation process, not only as a good sounding board, but also as changes in duties are made *everyone* can keep track of and adjust workloads as needed for a balanced workflow.

Be extra careful to also match the level of responsibility to the amount of authority. It can be easy to quickly assign anyone that you see with a spare minute to help.

For example, the front desk should *not* be looking at the bank account each day for automated clearing house (ACH) drafts to give to the billing department!

Some Delegation Ideas
to Prime the Pump:

- Identify key occurrences for delegation. You will find a rhythm. Meetings ... incentives ... initiative ... role changing ... new location ... Take note of employees that ask the best questions! They are already engaged and ready for more.

- If you feel like nothing can be delegated, then break it down. Try looking at tasks within the tasks that require the fewer skills.

- As you delegate, document clear objectives. Take the time to clarify the objectives: this will be important for you and the person you delegate the work to.

- Think about making a list of things to be done—just a list—with no solutions. After that, break it down among (1) what can be done tomorrow, (2) what needs to be done today, and (3) what someone else can do. This is prioritizing according to the level of expertise as well as the time when due.

- Remember that your role as a leader changes all the time as you are managing others. When focusing on *your* work and not micromanaging the work delegated, you have multiplied efforts versus just adding redundancy to a task.

- This is a great chance to get someone really excited about moving up and helping you at the same time.

- It is not uncommon for those who begin at the front desk or as a nurse assistant to seek opportunities to move up from their current position. It's a win-win situation when you recognize that initiative. Offer some tasks and/or projects that are appropriate along the way. Feed that and see where that ingenuity thrives.

Color and Scents Can Affect Performance and Attitude

As opportunities to re-design areas of your office arise, choose your color palette very intentionally. Even one wall of color in your office and lobby can make a huge impact on the emotional reactions of patients and staff.

I strongly recommend reserving more intense colors for areas where more of the action typically occurs. Conversely, plain colors can equally drag productivity down.

A brilliant color for any area is a deep jade green, deep butternut, or medium tinted blue. Happy colors are bright yellow, blue, pink, grass green, and orange.

A calming, relaxed palette would be soft light green, grey, sky and medium blue and even medium purples can ease the savage beast in all of us. Quiet colors are dark blues and purples and light pink. The approach I like that I believe makes a patient feel comfortable (and staff more productive) is to avoid yellow and red as they are excitement colors. They are not conducive to calming. When I am looking for a calming influence, sage green can satisfy as a balancing color. Blue is a healing color, and green is the color of balance.

Now, picture your office again. Consider your examination rooms, lobby, and even the office where payment arrangements are made. They should all match the purpose of the area and be conducive to the feeling that you want people to have as they enter and exit the room.

While medical practices often avoid scents out of courtesy, certain aromas may actually be beneficial in specific environments to calm you down or brighten your day. For example, bright scents are excellent for focusing on work, while lavender or chamomile may be more soothing when you want a less stressful and quieter atmosphere, such as counseling patients or family members.

Story

Is Coffee an Operating Supply or a Benefit?

Speaking of things that greatly affect operations, to many, including me, morning coffee is a vital part of a morning routine and getting the day started.

Our medical director liked to save money when and wherever he could, including the coffee made available to staff. He bought the cheapest coffee he could find; I would describe the taste as minimally bearable. It was requested that the practice purchase a better grade of coffee. His response was that no one could really tell one coffee from another. Talk about a morale killer!

As someone who takes her coffee very seriously, I volunteered to conduct a taste test to prove that there are very big differences between cheap and better coffee, and that I could identify them— no labels needed.

The physician did not believe I could tell the difference and took me up on that offer! A week or two later, there was an entire experiment set up in the conference room with four clear jars of aromatic coffee labeled A, B, C, and D. I was blindfolded, then I tasted the different coffees with the goal of determining which one tasted the best, as well as being able to identify the most and the least expensive.

The first one was easily and immediately distinguished, as it was an excellent coffee. I was also able to categorize the others as well. The physician graciously purchased better coffee, to the eternal gratitude of the staff.

Delegate, not Dump

Some may consider that delegating offers someone a chance to take initiative, sink their teeth into something new, and advance. But authority and respect are also important when dealing with staff in a delegation scenario. You must present yourself as respectable in the workplace, and not as someone just trying to pass off your work.

When describing the task to be delegated, don't say, "I just don't have the time for it." That makes it appear the task has little value and a lack of honor to the delegated staff members. Set a tone of respect when allocating. This also allows us to tap into staff members' previous work history, bringing out things such as working with reports or other tasks that you may regularly need assistance with.

There needs to be a commitment from the staff member for it to have a purpose beyond the request to be done. Explain how it will help and get a genuine buy-in. For example, running a report to gauge call back response timing will really help the practice balance the load amongst the nurses. Making sure the person taking on the task understand them will enable to work to feel more rewarding to them. To be able to envision the end result of any function and task is important.

If we are delegating to staff that are often multitasking, try to delegate similar activities to one person for an easier flow. Once interrupted, it can take several minutes to return to where we left off. An example of this would be scheduling monthly birthday celebrations, representative events, and patient education events.

When you say thank you, be specific as to *why* you are thanking them, and remember that the two things people like to hear most are *their name* and *thank you*.

How Can You Delegate Individually When Everyone Does Everything?

With everyone so busy, before becoming efficient, prioritize effectiveness.

Efficiency is when we do something quickly and well, but effectiveness determines processes chosen and how well you do it. It's no use being hyper efficient at a task that has little to no effectiveness. And there are those staff members that consistently look for the easiest tasks to do. This can result in an imbalance of duties among employees that can quickly turn to resentment and lower morale.

You are already approaching prioritizing in your world of juggling time.

Sort out the most important tasks and apply them directly to each person's role. That alone can define what each person does hopefully with an updated written job description to support that position. The job description then becomes a great training tool from which they can sign off on each task throughout the on boarding process. A great confirmer of thorough and specific training. It also serves as a confidence booster as the new employee sees exactly what is expected and goes for it!

One gentle reminder from an accounting major, as you change any role and policy, please also ensure that financial checks and balances sync with any new protocols.

Offer Education with Assignments

There is a plethora of resources that can be offered to staff for training. Along with webinars and onsite conferences, also consider in-house onsite training.

One of the benefits is that all staff members get the *same* message and trainers are usually as comfortable training 5 staff members as they are training 250 people in a room. When everyone hears the identical information, it forms a connection of understanding … something they learned together. We all had our classroom friends, right? It is also a relating experience. Envision staff members referencing each other as a personal resource to confirm or correct the best procedures and policies and what to do next. Create a positive learning environment that promotes education and communication among peers.

You can also often record the sessions for any future employees to be part of their on boarding process.

Trainings can be invigorating and fun as well as educational. One of my favorites is a corporate meeting where the staff gets involved with either communication and/or trust and customer service exercises. Role-playing between physicians and staff is almost always quite humorous and engaging. Real, topical, and practice-specific issues are able to be openly and honestly discussed. These are learning experiences that your staff will actually enjoy!

As you delegate:

◆ Set deadlines for everything, even small things. Sometimes we assign according to our terms, not theirs. It's a matter of clarity. ASAP may mean yesterday to you and three days to someone else.

◆ Informing the priority level is essential. They don't know how urgent the request is unless we let them know.

◆ Allow enough time to complete to *your* satisfaction for a successful set up and establish a realistic due date.

◆ Your best workers want you to see what they are doing.

The best delegators will tell you that the way they are able to do so is because if someone does not meet their role there will be a discussion about it. Someone seeking a professional career will welcome that conversation to improve.

Human Workflow Exercise

A fun and very telling exercise is to have all staff members grouped by department and standing in a single line. As you call out a task, such as a referral, each person steps forward explaining their part in the task. If it ends up looking like you're conducting a disorganized orchestra, there is probably room for improvement in there somewhere.

It truly points out who is doing what at every point and redundancies can be discovered as you go through this exercise. What processes can be streamlined? It's a lot of fun and also allows each person to shine and state their role and value within the practice. My guess is that you see some surprising things come out of it.

Managing the Change so that Everyone Can Change with It

There has to be a benefit to change to make it stick, and delegation can be a big change. Once someone sees and feels that benefit, they tend to do it even more! Why not? Rewards every time!

As you approach each step of change, clarify with questions that will help you define what the practice has achieved, what the practice wants, why the practice wants it, and exactly how to get there. What are the possible barriers that you may run across while trying to achieve the objective?

Practice-wide shared goals will help staff members maintain a momentum while getting the job done!

When following up, always be clear and concise with staff so all points are easily referenceable and documented.

"Intelligence is the ability to adapt to change."

Stephen Hawking

Employ periodic (no more than weekly, unless warranted) emails, especially for long-term tasks. With this updated information, you and your employee are given the opportunity to discuss and even improve developments along the way!

Successful delegation is a part of fruitful relationship management. You never do it alone. You need the commitment of many people to create the most effective communicative workforce and continued relationships that move you forward as an individual and the practice forward as a group.

Delegation also means releasing!

Nuances of Leadership That Effect Credibility

What Makes Us Tick and the Essential Characteristics for Success

> *"Do one thing every day that scares you."*
>
> *Eleanor Roosevelt*
>
> *(My daughter gave me a mug with this quote on it. She said she gave it to me because I do this every day. What a compliment!)*

Establishing a Level of Mindful Professionalism

Some of us are fortunate enough to know what we want to "grow up to be" from a very early age. My husband knew he wanted to be in the arts, and my sister always knew she wanted to be in medicine. I was an art major that didn't really have a clue as to what I would do first, let alone a long-term goal. I took an accounting course in college and fell in love with numbers. Who would have thought?

While hard work and chance may place us in certain positions, it is a wonderful idea to have goals in mind. For those who are considering and on the edge of management, please deliberate the following pointers so you may be more than prepared as the opportunity presents.

Listen. Pay attention. And not just to conversations and people, but listen to the practice, the rhythm and routine as a whole. Notice the dynamics for the pulse of the practice. Who tends to be the loner? Who tends to have the most concerns?

Be aware of the key players, their future plans and goals of the practice. See who asks the most questions and seems to be the most involved.

To be on the ground floor and a part of any project can be very exciting as well as propel you into a newly created position that you help shape.

Troubleshoot potential issues. No one can make everyone happy all the time, but we can certainly make a difference. Also be aware of employees and potential future issues. For example, does everyone have the physical space needed? I once worked in an office where the front desk had just enough room for two chairs and computers. That's it—not even room for a copier. I have seen larger cubbyholes. I don't know how they did it.

Staff are often a very positive and supportive influence as you create your imprint upon the practice. Invite honesty and let them know that you invite their feedback with no repercussions. How wonderful if you can accept them for who they are! Staff members will appreciate that and hopefully speak up even more and connect, which is so important. This is a win-win situation as you direct and build a loyal hard-working team.

Though my transition into administration was a welcome one, I was still quite surprised. But the level of acceptance of such a new position can be very different when it is not a desired one. Whether due to emergency or other circumstances, when a leadership role is unexpectedly thrust upon you, you may have more trouble with the changeover. This is sometimes referred to as being an "accidental" manager.

Sometimes I wonder if these unanticipated leaders were actually meant to be following a natural flow that others already saw them filling that or a similar role. Many of those elevated to an unantici-pated post are often long-time employees with a proven work history and trusted relationships throughout the practice and community. If this is your situation, take that and run with it. What a perfect start to a new position!

As true with any new rule, you will need some additional knowledge to fill in gaps. Excellent leadership calls for learning additional skills to completely fulfill the role. Administrators have the most incredible single impact on staff retention and engagement. The role is beyond important.

If you are not as familiar with the total goings-on at the practice, here are a few tips to get you immersed in operations and help gain staff engagement.

Tip #1

Your job as an administrator clearly includes managing relation-ships. Take the time to sit down with each of your staff members for at least one to two hours. Focus on communicating in a totally transparent way as you begin a relationship and build rapport and trust. Review their job description and ask for feedback. Are there any tools needed? Do they need more training or more to do? (You would be surprised how many want more to do.)

Tip #2

Observe and assess positions and staff. When you finish, you will see distinct patterns and may even "have the whole picture." You will create a connection and affirm their value as you spend time with the employees. From here, you are able to move more com-prehensively with different perspectives in mind as practice-wide initiatives are introduced.

Tip #3

If you are not already involved in financial activity, have a clear understanding of financial checks and balances, reporting, and your budget.

Tip #4

With physicians, have one-on-one meetings as well as a group meeting so you may understand and reinforce the practice mission and priorities.

Tip #5

Being transparent and admitting when you make mistakes is great for staff to see. We are all human and it is okay (and inevitable) to make mistakes. If you have not already, educate yourself on emotional intelligence. Self-awareness and relationship management offers empathy that will take you far when communicating and interacting with staff, physicians, and patients.

Every one of us has our own experiences and stories on how we were first introduced and started in administration. And sometimes it is funny how we end up somewhere. There have been times when there has been an opening and I thought, "It may as well be me!" And I went for it. These can be great experiences and positive moves to learn and move forward.

My first position in a medical office was definitely a life transition for me. I was fortunate enough to be able to remain home until my children were at ages where I was comfortable going back to work. It was incredibly hard, but I knew it would be a good move for me. After working in tax and public accounting, I sought a job in the little town where my children went to school. I found a position in a medical office doing their accounting work and being at the front desk from three o'clock to five o'clock. Needless to say, I learned a lot!

Moving up or to management was not important to me at that point. My priority was maintaining a great family life and a good job. In that order. I never thought about it as a career until a physician assistant found a prior administrator's door sign and stuck it on my door, saying to me, "We know what you do and thank you."

While unanticipated, it was a welcome thought and my immediate intuition was that I needed to know a lot more! While I had a great deal of working experience and an accounting degree, I still lacked medical managerial and administrative training. When first working with other managers, I depended upon my common sense and "street smarts." I continually learned from them, I listened, we worked together, and the staff responded positively. To be honest, I needed support, and they needed a good leader. It was a great relationship where teamwork was a natural progression.

When handling physician concerns and supervising staff members, I built my knowledge base as I built a team. Fortunately, I had the overall backing of an incredible staff and ended up managing the practice for ten years!

For another perspective, there were a few hard lessons. Your confidence will always be rewarded with more work to do. In other words, the demand for our time and efforts will always exceed our time available … think about it … or else we would not have a job.

There are times when being in charge will push your boundaries and values of what is easiest or preferable and what is right. You will have to know the difference between empathy and when someone is trying to take advantage of a situation. This often requires you to make tough decisions and stand for what you believe in. This is where emotional intelligence respects one's ethical values and maintaining a culture of respect.

You have made it to management! Be ready to balance more than you ever have before. Your role and other roles too!! Your time is at a premium and extremely valuable. There will now always be a "professional line" and new boundaries to be established between you and former co-workers and peers now that you are in "management."

Do not feel the need to speak with people differently. You can build upon any already well-known rapport and connection, continuing in a very positive direction. Your words are important, and staff is listening. Use your words wisely to inspire and promote. It's okay to re-establish boundaries and connections, just on a different level.

Staff recalibrating to changes is continual and may escalate with managerial changes. Our animal instincts make many of us naturally territorial, and that may shift. We all like to know where we stand. Do not be surprised if the performance of the team drops through a transition phase. This is a normal reaction and will improve as you complete and reinforce staff members position within the practice. If you are honest and show your support and hard work for the entire practice and every staff member, it will show. Authenticity and sincerity go a long way. Allow them to envision a future where they are valued and watch as they relax (just a little bit) as a new routine and standards are set.

If more assistance or specific expertise is warranted, sincere leaders are confident in asking for help. No one is 100 percent trained in everything. There's absolutely nothing wrong with turning to professionals when needed. There are projects where it is much better to have someone who can come in and do it better and faster so that you are able to fulfill your role and keep the practice running smoothly.

I worked with a wonderful practice where the billing manager had recently been moved up to the administrator. The request for an assessment included, "I don't know what I don't know." We worked together for a few days and discovered that, overall, with some fill-in-the-gap projects and a few attitudes to adjust, she had been doing a stellar job. We worked on some projects together, and she was all set. What great affirmation for someone new to the role—and she learned a lot through the process.

One of the most important things to remember, as I often tell my kids, is that no matter what you're doing, if you are learning something, you are also moving forward. There is always a new way to look at and possibly improve things.

When you find yourself in positions that you may or may not expect and make the best of it, options will continue to present themselves if you look for and tap into your resources. Part of your professional progression is to explore any and all options. A true leader keeps going with the utmost integrity and completes the job to the best of their ability.

Even if this is not your final goal, keep in mind that you were placed in this position because you are qualified, and someone believes that you can carry this out. Transfer that affirmation into confidence in the most positive way as you fulfill your new role. Where you go from here is up to you!

Mentors

It is always good to have a mentor and now could be perfect timing. Mentors are a true gift that encourage and guide with major life and professional decisions. If you are lucky enough to have one (or more), they are a gold mine of support that has lifelong impact. They touch a note in you that makes it personal and caring and supportive all at once. They are a treasure.

It is a wonderful idea for everyone to seek one as they enter practice management, just someone to touch base with and firmly establish that first connection with the practice. That mentorship may indeed blossom into a deeper professional rapport as well.

My most impactful mentor, Sylvia Icenhour, actually led my certification study group. As with many advisers, she encouraged us with an undying confidence that we could all attain the certification anytime we wanted to, using our already gained knowledge. After a time, we had all received certification and fellowship, and I remain in touch with most members of the group.

"There is no normal life that is free of pain. It's the very wrestling with our problems that can be the impetus for our growth."

Fred Rogers

But Sylvia and I just kept going. We further developed our friendship and would discuss professional decisions. She offered the pluses and minuses of each choice, and we have a beautiful relationship. To this day, I call her whenever I make a major decision. She is a phenomenal woman and is a most positive example for anyone seeking in improving their professionalism. It is always good to have someone that really knows us and offers that extra level of support that can help balance priorities and look at things through different lenses. Thank you, Sylvia!

Get it Done! The Three "D's"

Completing projects can be quite challenging for many reasons. We can have the *best* ideas, but we also need ambition and implementation! Some say that leaders have the ability to progress with or without general consensus. And there are also times we really need to get something done but can't quite gather the motivation to move forward.

There are three "D's" to change, commitment, and carrying it through. They are desire, decision, and discipline.

Think about instances when you have had to do something (either personal or for business) that is difficult to get started, let alone complete! There are many things we know that we should do, but it is the decision and discipline that make it happen.

Approaching in steps may help launch the mental build up essential for continual discipline. Look up from your desk and walk around the office, even the lobby and staff room, (yes, right now if you have 5 minutes) and note projects large and small, a wish list if you will, that helps you immediately identify your priorities to start with that you would like to tackle but have not yet been able to take the next step.

It's important to put these in writing so you are looking at what is needed; that makes it a little more difficult to rationalize why they cannot be done! Sometimes just taking that first step in getting started is all we need. If it's still difficult, then begin with the smallest and easiest goal. Acknowledge and realize the value you will derive from completing this, hopefully moving onto the next project with positive outcomes in mind.

Story

Okay, I Admit It

When my daughter was twelve years old, she asked why I volunteer for so many things. My response to her was spontaneous and clearly relayed the desire to control my environment: "I would rather be part of the process and help define the standards than to have to follow someone else's rules that I may not agree with."

It was a simple and honest truth that I am okay with. Protecting your surroundings is a natural instinct. Many like to establish their own preferred parameters. And there's nothing wrong with that! Especially when it benefits everyone and reaps positive results.

Promoted from Peer to Manager? You Are One of *Them* Now!

Talk about nuances that affect credibility! Consider being well-established in one role and then promoted to executive level. Boom! You are now "One of them."

The biggest challenge for you may be how to wear your new "hat" among co-workers that used to be your friends, and now you are their boss! Managers work on behalf of the practice, and that is the defining line as you consider appropriateness of conversations. People now look to you as the practice representative. This can tip the scales and dynamics even with an already-formalized and excellent rapport. It is no longer about you and your individual contributions to the practice. Regarding individual communications, some employees may now be unsure as to your disposition, and they may also have concerns about the need to possibly approach you in a different manner.

Your work is also now judged by your team's success not just your individual efforts.

If you approach this directly, each conversation will help rebalance your relationship. Start listening, talking … and listening!

As I mentioned earlier, my management background began with seeking a job to be near my children's school so I could continue to volunteer with their activities. A family practice with obstetrics needed a practice accountant and someone to help at the front desk. I am sure many will agree there is no experience like the front desk—and I mean really working the front desk, not just visiting once in a while.

"If you think you are too small to make a difference, try sleeping with a mosquito."

Tenzin Gyatso, The 14th Dalai Lama

Within a year, I was promoted to manager and suddenly found myself being "one of them." Even though it was just a few who treated me differently, it was still surprising and an awakening.

Remember too (and this is important at three o'clock in the morning) that you are never alone. As I said, my promotion was my first management position, and I was very inexperienced. There is support and camaraderie. A few months into my new management position, a nurse known lovingly known to the entire community as "Miss Annie" said, "You know, I wasn't sure how you would be as a manager. But when I saw you had the whole practice in mind, I knew it would be okay." I loved it, and she made me feel like I was definitely heading in the right direction and really added to my confidence. We still talk today.

Managers look at the entire practice in totality: every staff member, every office, and every department.

With a slight transition in approach, tapping into your emotional intelligence enables you to handle things on a higher level of professionalism. You do not react, you respond.

Trust yourself. This is why you are in this position and it's okay to be in charge. Reproduce the same characteristics that most likely brought you to this point and fine tune where needed. My guess is that just being yourself and do what you've been doing all along is a great start. Enjoy the ride!

Flip a Challenging Characteristic into a Gift

Sometimes our limitations or personal barriers can in turn work to our advantage. People who are impulsive tend to live in the moment and can be great promoters and marketers. Some people may be seen as pushy, but they are often the ones that see that doing something right takes a little extra effort sometimes.

Someone who may appear to have limited knowledge of something is also free from preoccupation with previously determined attitudes. Someone who talks too much is often extremely passionate about their ideas and interests.

Thomas is a gentleman that I met at my first job following college. He knew everything about classical music, was a concert pianist, and highly autistic. His job was delivering the mail throughout the entire hospital. He was a personable, wonderful man and absolutely perfect for the job. We would see each other and walk together. I would quickly become engrossed in his discussions of classical music. He was also a true gentleman. Thomas retired after 20 years of dedicated service to the hospital and community. As with any situation, let's make the best of each person's natural predispositions.

Story

Making it Work at Work

There was a practice where one of the clinical staff was a pathological liar. This person was very nice, but, for whatever reasons, they simply could not help themselves. If they told a story, it was usually less than truthful. When this person was placed as a department manager, I expressed my concerns to the medical director. I was certain the department would suffer.

The decision was not changed, and I had to live with it. This new department manager and I had nothing in common, and I did not trust anything that was said.

Nonetheless, I knew I needed to establish some kind of rapport, as neither of us were going anywhere. The practice's success is always my ultimate concern. I found one thing we had in common that would allow us to converse on a more familiar level. Based upon that we built a rapport and worked together in a more comfortable, as well as professional, manner for many years.

Characteristics of Successful Leaders

All kinds of people become leaders, and yet there are certain characteristics that leaders seem to have as a common thread. For example, leaders tend to plan ahead for difficult times. Leaders look at big projects and little tasks. As Grandma said, we see "the whole picture." Also, our passion and dedication to patient care continually grows, building momentum and serving as a catalyst for change. And we love it!

No matter what your position is at this moment, you are learning and investing in a well-rounded knowledge that can only help in your future. Take your time and explore and find what charges you the most. This is where, as you explore different tangents of healthcare, you will find the parts that really energize you and where you really feel that calling. For me, I love helping everyone do their job better, and they feel really good about being there every day making a valued contribution.

It can be very exciting to be part of monumental changes! We know that healthcare, as in many industries, is changing every moment. If we stand still even for a moment, we are already behind, and we love surging forward!

Awareness and Emotional Intelligence

Cultivating awareness in this context is understanding and controlling your own emotional state and realizing how you and your staff look to your patients. Emotional intelligence is something that affects every relationship you have and is essential for your credibility and success.

Those with emotional intelligence are able to admit mistakes, take personal responsibility, and hold others accountable as well. They are also able to listen without jumping to assumptions.

I found the information provided by the Institute for Health and Human Potential, in the executive summary section of their white paper, "The Business Case for Emotional Intelligence," incredibly important.

> Research shows that people who work for emotionally intelligent managers and leaders choose to give more than what is asked of them in their job (discretionary effort) driving overall organization engagement. In a recent worldwide survey, we found that 43 percent of employees agree or strongly agreed that "if my manager has more emotional intelligence, I will give extra effort." [23]

Superior Communication Skills

It is of supreme importance for leaders to have the ability to speak clearly and be completely understood.

Communication is being responsible for listening and being aware! The word has evolved from the Latin word *communis*, which means "to share." Communication is the act of conveying meanings from one entity or group to another through understood signs. Communications should be viewed as a strategic imperative for high performance and growth. They can bring creative skills and empathy, functioning with firsthand knowledge of sought-after results.

Now, think about all the different ways you communicate verbally and nonverbally every day. And consider how you may employ your professional ability to relay appropriate authority with respect. You also utilize resources directing communications in support of practice objectives in the most positive way. It's all about the end goal and what is best for the practice. This is also where personal or professional ethics may enter the picture.

Looking Beyond Biases

Most of us are intuitively drawn to certain types of people. They might be similar to us, finding instant commonalities, which can make it very easy to develop a rapport. Acceptance is a deep and needed desire present in all of us. Moving beyond those we have an easy time connecting with can be a tremendously difficult challenge. You may have to make extra effort to focus on cultivating an appreciation for people who think, act, and feel differently than you.

It is your job to always challenge yourself. You will seldom achieve anything great if you only interact with people who are in your comfort zone. You need creativity and challenging scenarios for progressive and positive energy, Great progress requires disruptive ideas and talents to come together in sometimes unanticipated ways.

Cultural Awareness

Cultural awareness is a necessity and a very special and much appreciated sensitivity. Every practice says they are just like a family, which is true. What is also true is that every family has its dynamics.

For example, beginning a new job, you need to learn how things are done within that atmosphere, correct? This knowledge is eventually gained if you are even halfway aware, as a lot of this is filling in between the lines can occur just from being there for a few months.

There also may be times when you are working with someone who is culturally different than you. Becoming familiar with those individual aspects begins the bonding and common courtesies for each other.

Paul King, MD, CEO of Children's Health of Stanford may have said it best:

> The more experience you have with a diverse group of colleagues, the more you will learn that people don't look at the same issues in the same way. Men and women are different. There are different cultures. Diversity is more than skin deep. It's diversity of thought and diversity of economic background. All those things bring a richness of experience to solving problems that a singular way of thinking just does not provide.[24]

Performance Request?
It's Not Personal

"When haters go after your looks and differences, it means they have nowhere left to go—and then you know you're winning! I have Asperger's and that means I'm sometimes a bit different from the norm. And given the right circumstances, being different is a superpower."

Greta Thunberg

Asking someone to perform better is not necessarily a personal attack, but it can be hard to differentiate and accept. Managers work on behalf of the physicians and practice and in a perfect world are viewed as such. We are human and have emotions, so sometimes it's impossible for such a discussion not to be taken personally.

There was a point where I needed to tell a close friend of mine that she was not pulling her weight and missing a lot of deadlines (notice I say friend instead of employee. I had very recently been promoted to manager).

I felt so torn, that at the end, I actually began to apologize. She said, "I wouldn't respect you unless you said something. I'm glad that you did." It's always good to have an experience that clearly defines the lines for you.

The encounter was enlightening in that you don't have to take it personally and you can focus on what the practice needs most.

There will be times when your staff helps you draw boundaries without realizing it. Thank you, Valerie.

Employees Want to Know …

Below I list questions that each and every person in every position has at one point or another. Your answer should be a resounding "Yes!" to all of them. Affirmation of someone's value in the practice should be embedded and a part of an employee's everyday interactions with management.

Does my opinion matter to you?

Yes! That is why we have general staff meetings as well as departmental committees to openly discuss staff member experiences and suggestions.

When are you going to ask me about the new EMR?

As we select new systems such as practice management or other process driven services, each staff member's voice is incremental to our operational workflow.

How are you going to make me feel that my job is important?

We can acknowledge an employee's value many different ways. Everything from a gold star to place on their ID tag to gift certificates and awards to help one feel the importance of their role within the practice. And when one of the physicians formally recognizes the employee, it makes it that much sweeter!

What am I doing right and wrong so I can progress in my job?

Hopefully, between an annual evaluation and periodic one on ones, the progress and goals have been established and feedback is received regularly.

In the recent past, have I been offered any ways to improve my work or move forward in the practice?

Even with our offering of continual growth in any position, it is also up to the employee to seek out opportunities to improve their performance and grow their position. That's resourcefulness.

"My mission in life is not merely to survive, but to thrive; and to do so with some passion, some compassion, some humor, and some style."

Maya Angelou

Feedback

Feedback is always needed, in a good way! While feedback is so important to receive with what we can improve as well as what we are doing well, keep in mind that negativity breeds negativity and positive energy is always a good thing.

Researchers at the University of Chicago, led by Lauren Eskreis-Winkler, designed an experiment to identify whether positive feedback or negative feedback resulted in improved learning. Eskreis-Winkler and her team state in their study results published in the journal *Psychological Science* that:

> Our society celebrates failure as a teachable moment, Yet we find that failure does the opposite: it undermines learning. Failure feedback undermines learning motivation because it is ego threatening. It causes participants to tune out and stop processing information. Our key result is that people find failure feedback ego threatening, which leads them to tune out, and miss the information it offers. In other words, failure undermines learning.[25]

As published on *Inc.com*, Lee Colan offers this insight, "Today's technology and social media platforms enable us to express top-of-mind, unfiltered thoughts to the world—often to disastrous results. Remember, just because we can say something doesn't mean we should." Whoever is offering the feedback, or any other participation, please consider the following as you formulate your contribution or response:

THINK

T. Is it *true?*

H. Is it *helpful?*

 (or is it just criticism that will have no positive outcome?)

I. Is it *inspiring?*

N. Is it *necessary?*

K. Is it *kind* and conveyed with good intentions? We can offer suggestions in a pleasant constructive manner.[26]

Handling A Limited Culture

There are practices that follow unspoken policies that are probably costing more than they may be aware of. "We have always done it this way," and "We hire within a certain profile," and "Things will never change," are their mantras. Closed cultures tend not to welcome new ideas or theories of management as they go directly against everything they have learned in their experiences with that practice.

If we accept limited parameters, we become stuck. And, again, consider that it's always easier to hire someone you know or one who sees things the same way you do. I have also worked with practices that tend to hire friends and or family members. I believe this can be an issue if carried too far and actually work against continual growth. It can be a rude awakening when they are unable to retain employees and the patient base becomes stagnant.

For example, a new manager comes in that has absolutely incredible ideas never heard before and very different from the culture that has been created. Anticipated changes are one thing, sudden change is another and can take anyone by surprise.

It is best when individuals within their role as well as the practice as a group are invited to be innovative. Every practice needs to sustain healthy growth with a resilient, forward thinking presence benefiting the patients and community.

10

The Provider's Mindfulness— Trust and Support, Relationships and Resolutions

"You rarely have time for everything you want in this life, so you need to make choices. And hopefully your choices can come from a deep sense of who you are."

Fred Rogers

As stated in the beginning of this book, the relationship between the physician and administrator is a partnership of care, leading the practice through success and growth, as well as hard times and unexpected challenges. It is truly close to marriage in that it is a relationship that recognizes a professional union of values and work ethic. As leaders, when times are tough, we should tap into that unity and elevated level of dedication to the practice. There are many incredibly committed staff, and I am not discounting any employee's loyalty or devotion.

Of course, administrators and physicians may not agree, which highlights even more the need for a respectful and communicative rapport. Very simply, we have to know how to communicate our ideas and visions in the best way possible as well as listen to other's approaches. Gaining familiarity will allow us to use our emotional intelligence skills in the most useful ways that matter the most.

If the Manager is New to the Practice or New Providers?

I suggest you start at the top to find the most important practice-wide missions and priorities. My first meeting is always with the providers as a group to establish these parameters.

Then take the time to get to know each one on an individual basis. This is the beginning foundation of your connection and bond. No matter how many providers you have, this pays back on a multitude of levels.

Picking the location for your first individual meeting is a strategic decision. It is likely that they are most comfortable in their own secure environment, thus meeting with each physician in their office (not yours) is most preferable.

If there are no private offices, allow them to suggest an alternate location that affords them the control to opt for an atmosphere most comfortable for them. Bonding can begin here, consequently hastening the process of confident reliance on you!

This person is now the center of your universe. Listen first; this is their time with you. As soon as you discover that first common link ... the trust has begun.

Lean towards them, take notes, ask questions, and write down the answers.

When done, the seeds of faith in you have been planted. And the icing on the cake? You have a true understanding of the practice's, as well as individual providers', priorities. What a great example of another win-win-win situation!

Whatever your approach, sincerity is always essential. A forced concern or compliment is usually seen through, with the rest of the conversation then possibly received with a grain of salt.

As we help lead physicians and staff in decision-making, they will see the results of changes made, share in the ownership of that adjustment and look to you as the leader that brought it all together.

Respect the history preceding you as you are establishing your own footprint within the practice. The previous administrator's "presence" can also work against you if it sticks around too long. Meeting with managers and key staff will help you establish a transitional relationship, while taking time to understand the complete practice dynamics and building upon your relationships.

"I am just a child who has never grown up. I still keep asking these 'how' and 'why' questions. Occasionally, I find an answer."

Stephen Hawking

Conflicts (and Resolutions)

Working Through an In-House Dispute

Initially, the manager is the gatherer of information from providers and staff that may be involved. This is a dispassionate process, no gasps, emotion, or any kind of behavior that may reflect taking a particular opinion or side should be shown. Remember that all employees observe you at least some time during your day. A pattern of conduct resembling provider unhappiness can affect morale quickly and deeply. Attain maximum privacy by meeting with appropriate staff members before or after hours or away from "office ears."

Once you have all the information, the next course of action depends upon your practice's structure as to what is most appropriate. It could be a managing physician, a medical director, or a board of directors.

This is also one of those times to consider bringing in an attorney or other professional to help assess and determine the best approach in resolving the situation.

As the one in charge, it is the manager's responsibility to cover all the bases, aware of any contractual and/or legal implications that may occur as a result of the provider conflict.

The next meeting is crucial. It can set the tone for a healing environment that respects the practice hierarchy while not interrupting patient care and maintaining staff morale. Have a witness present only if you feel you must do so to reduce the "intimidation" factor.

Unspoken Conflict

Like all of us, sometimes physicians do not communicate their problems with peers and staff. Also, of no surprise, it can affect the staff and morale before reaching the point where the manager actually approaches it.

To be able to address such a conflict respectfully, this is the time to play facilitator and peacemaker, first meeting individually with each person involved. Sometimes it is simply a matter of conveying one provider's frustration to another because they do not know what else to do and need a little guidance.

Other times it can be much more serious and, if not handled, everything can quickly go into a negative spin. One example, when one provider works harder than another, yet earns less. Ownership, call time, payer mix, schedules, patient flow can all be contributors.

Keep the provider apprised and involved as you determine what is occurring. Then as the leader, you bring it all together to facilitate finding a balance to a fairer formula.

This type of conflict can grow and grow if not addressed, until, one day, that aggrieved provider says they are leaving, partially because nothing was done. Taking the time to really tune in to the undercurrents as well being available for vocalized issues can avoid such a drastic cost to the practice. Taking control of a problem to protect the practice.

External Disagreement

Depending upon the circumstances, a team approach may be more appropriate with a problem that arises due to an event or relationship with a person or entity outside of the practice. One example may be another practice or a payer. No matter the issue, when the problem goes outside of the practice, your reputation can be at stake.

One illustration, if a payer threatens to terminate a contract or a major insurance audit goes poorly, you want to protect and correct so you may resume a successful agreement and maintain continuity in patient care. Additional scenarios could be a difference of opinion regarding call coverage or general standards of care.

It is crucial for everyone to take part in gathering information and determining next best steps as soon as possible The goal is to have a unified group approach to any situation. If you think it will help, also call in the reinforcements: your staff! Clue them in as to how they can assist. Trust me, the staff knows something is up most of the time. Let them be a part of the solution and add to the loyalty factor. Pride comes from ownership of a job well done—let all involved share in that!

You may need to meet with other administrators and/or other physicians involved in the process. Meet often with a committee of key players that can most help achieve positive results and keep an eye on things until long after it has seemed to be resolved to be aware of any repercussions beyond the event.

Have one final bringing-it-all together meeting and report final results to the physicians. Once again, as a leader, you have safeguarded the practice while facilitating providers in resolving an issue affecting everyone. And be sure to stay in tune for any more damage control or fine-tuning that may need to be done as a follow up.

To manage the problem, reviewing the history and pertinent information will help in providing up to three possible solutions. You are "Switzerland," remaining neutral while offering the facts.

This is also a time when it is good for providers to talk it out if possible. What is said in the boardroom stays in the boardroom. There has to be total trust in the confidentiality of these conversations. And no recording of such sessions!

It can be challenging not to have a peer to talk to confidentially about the details. We all need to let it out sometimes. What differentiates us as leaders is that we are concerned with the whole of the group and must maintain privacy, always looking forward and protecting the honor of the practice.

One example is to participate in retreats, more private one-on-one meetings, and maybe even send a physician to "charm school." There are many successful approaches for physicians that have only positive results with peers, staff, and even patients. Fortunately, we have successfully brought it all back together. Hopefully all agree that a positive result is the one we all prefer. The provider's choice to be responsible and take a part in the resolution is key!

Staff Barriers (Personal Dynamics)

With any practice, no matter how large or small, there should be a formal and structured hierarchy, including communications regarding who reports to who. The more layers of miscommunications, the greater potential for conflicting messages conveyed to staff, who may then simply make their own determination on how they would like to handle the issue.

A well-known and still popular challenge can be when a staff member goes directly to a physician instead of their manager or administrator with their problem. Respecting the practice hierarchy is a basic essential for several reasons. It can be undermining when such a lack of respect is shown. It also shows that the provider plays "favorites," which quickly affects morale in a negative manner. This is also immediately rendering the administrator powerless, a qualified and proficient person hired to administrate the practice. Respecting and trusting professional staff to carry out their role will further confirm and strengthen the structure of the practice as a whole. Specific allowances have their place, but a solid foundation of support is what carries it through.

"I'll Take Care of It"

Physicians love it when you take something off their plate! And you take great pride in getting it done!

Blend these excellent (and sometimes unexpected) opportunities to reiterate the common connection of excellent patient care and go from there. "I'll take care of it," is a favorite phrase of mine. It is almost like when you say to a patient, "I am trying to help you." They seem to reevaluate and relax, waiting for you to do your thing.

Too Much Trust?

There was a popular show called M.A.S.H. where a corporal, known as "Radar," would hold a piece of paper in front of his boss saying, "Sign this, please." And his boss would do so without looking.

I was *so* proud that my lead physician would do the same for me. I absolutely loved that he trusted me, saw me totally in charge making great decisions for the practice.

He always supported me, but leaders protect the practice in every way. I should *not* have allowed that. Beyond checks and balances, it is our role to define the boundaries as well as maintain a level of equilibrium. This does not weaken our stance and position as the leader of the practice. In fact, it reinforces our role, as these boundaries display respect for providers who now may perceive us more as a peer and professional.

Consistent Communication

Considering the seeming lack of anything long term in healthcare (anything more than 5 minutes), being able to know what needs to be relayed to the providers is hard enough to target. Couple that with the challenge of helping keep the provider's eyes on the end result, and you can begin to feel very stretched thin.

The key to surviving this reality is consistent, open communication. Start with a retreat and develop a one-, three- or five-year plan, a static meeting agenda topic, even a wish list. *Anything* that gets your providers motivated and going! You know the buttons to push to get them excited about their "carrot." What would they like to see happen? What do they see in their future? Let's see how we can make that happen.

A first sign of a natural leader is that we somehow always wind up being the "go to" person and the ones who get things done! It is our role to carry out the physician's goals and objectives every day. When staff supports physicians and physicians respect staff, it is a true partnership of care and patients notice that.

Peer Support and Professionalism

As you administrate your practice, also remember to keep nourishing your professionalism. Associate with your peers as much as possible through medical manager organizations, chambers of commerce, and other local and specialty organizations that can make you better as a whole. Sometimes we need to confirm that what we are doing is the best way possible, but it is just as exciting an opportunity to discover what we can work on a little more!

Look Around the Room

Who knows the ebb and flow of our lives almost as much as our family? Our co-workers. We are usually familiar with their attitude, habits, some beliefs, values, and behaviors. We all see the good, the bad, and the beautiful in each of us eventually. This is where common courtesies and awareness come into play. It is a simple and common respect for each other as we heal patients

Apply the time spent together to build upon co-worker rapport and staff members you can trust. You can build professionalism as a team or on an individual basis. The key is to progress professionally on every level with the full support of physicians and watch the practice fly!

11

Summary

Each of us has our own stories and history. In whatever way we begin, we make conscious choices along the way. Our work ethic begins with our first job and our first boss, and we move on from there. As my mom said, "I am the only person that has to live with myself the rest of my life."

Think of where you were five years ago or even a year ago. How different is your life right now?

When I was the writing this volume, I thought about my history with leadership.

There are times when I have accepted an unanticipated position because someone was going to be in that seat, so it may as well be me. Each time it has rewarded me in ways I never thought possible. We never know what is just around the corner.

For your own professional development, never stop looking at prospects and possibilities. As I continue to develop my skills, I am always looking for new approaches that can help me be a better person and leader. You will find that exposure to these options and actually exploring them will help you either confirm that you are where you should be or that there's a lot more that you would like to see! Either one is okay!

For my professional life, I have learned that I can love my job and know that it's also okay to find time to reflect and rejuvenate. There are times when everyone needs a little affirmation that they are doing the right thing and to find the right sources for encouragement to move forward in a productive and meaningful manner. Find those people. Be that person!

I value staff members more than ever with each step. I count on honest feedback and treasure their input in creating an office culture I am proud to be a part of. Emotional intelligence helps me relay that awareness with superior communication and relationship skills.

The best part? I am able to tune into my emotional intelligence, stand back, and be more observant than ever before. This helps me identify and appreciate what is working well as much as seeing other protocols and attitudes that may need some extra attention.

Remember to keep the "heart" in every major decision. There is nothing more important than your role in healing and caring for patients. Every experience should be focused on and begin with the most important relationship of the physician and patient. Everything is cultivated from there.

This is where a culture is created and upheld by your best team players. We all work together, from the C-suite to medical records. It is imperative for good leaders to recognize the value of each and every staff member as we hire and create a culture of bonding and pride. That's what makes teams work!

You should always be looking for the next step. Use emotional intelligence to help define a most aware, empathetic, and positive future.

Leadership works when different spectrums are combined to create a quality of care like no other.

Complete leadership in healthcare means being involved with every step and level of patient care offered. As we have learned, how the patient sees the front desk can affect how they may view the rest of their care: processes and protocols are intertwined and dependent upon each other for best practices and work and patient flow.

This first book is a great bridge towards the other two volumes of the trilogy. The next is about the soul of medicine—every facet of and perspective about the essential relationship between the patient and physician. The third volume then takes that relationship and adds it to the collaboration of care between the physician and administration and staff, which creates a synergy of care.

Let this writing serve as contribution towards achieving emotional intelligence in all areas of a management and leadership.

12

Vital Questions Posed to Some of My Favorite Executives

Throughout the years I have met incredible individuals, and as I thought about the content, I also wanted to include opinions of those I value the most. Below are a few examples of my favorite administrators and CEOs and their experiences.

I am so honored to add their viewpoints on these most important topics. Thank you!

LeeAnne Garms, CEO of Raleigh Neurology is someone who impresses you with her well-spoken and heartfelt words as much as her clear ability and experience in fulfilling her role

June McKernan, COO of Patient Preferred Dermatology Medical Group is incredibly intelligent, beyond creative with everything she does, business and personal. She is most respectful, professional and has one of the biggest hearts I've ever seen.

Linda ClenDening MS, FACMPE, CEO of Palm Beach Orthopedic Institute is a take charge person who keeps the patient front and center with every consideration and is a true professional.

Cinderella Tollefsen, MBA, FACMPE, CEO of Alaska Health Services is an active, warm, and enormously devoted professional that you can tell is capable of anything.

Anne Hill, MBA, FACMPE, CEO of Gastroenterology Associates of The Piedmont is a balanced blend of professionalism and pride, with an observant heart and gatherer of information.

She loves her role and is dedicated to accessible care for everyone everywhere.

Q: As a new CEO, what are the first things you would do upon entering the practice?

A: Cinderella

- Listen
- Observe
- Talk (with key folks)
- Understand current systems (before changing them)

A: June

- A life changing step would be to do "Insightful Discovery," a psychometric tool based on Carl Jung's psychology and energy. It utilizes a personality key that highlights 4 different colors that you can associate with behaviors and preferences. This will help greatly with learning how to communicate with others and how to approach in the best and most positive manner.

- Have a strategic business plan with owners, staff every employee. They should have goals and action items with accountability that can then be measured. Also realize that everything is adjustable and needs to be reasonable.

- Network and build your business relationships. We all need someone that is honest with us, that we can count on and know that they can count on you. These associates help you develop leadership traits that can be learned and empower others with enthusiasm.

A: Anne

- Assess the practice
- Be visible
- Meet everyone

◆ Listen!

◆ Look for an early win—a problem to solve

Q: *What are three pieces of advice you would offer a new CEO?*

A: **LeeAnn**

1. Find a personal board/group of people who will be honest with you.

2. Time is finite, a rare and precious resource as you are now pulled in even more directions. So, begin each day with a purpose that enables you clear goals that are a good start for the day. You may not succeed with all every day, but at least have embarked with a clear agenda.

3. The most important and biggest is that if you don't have the courage to fail, find it and use it wisely.

A: **Cinderella**

1. Never assume conspiracy when ignorance will do.

2. It's okay to take a pause before making a decision—especially on HR matters. Take time to get the other side of each story.

3. Trust your gut. You earned your position for a reason. Trust yourself.

A: **Linda**

1. Start with listening.

2. Respond with "I'll research and get back to you," if something is unknown—then be sure to follow through

3. Work as a servant to your patients, your staff and your physicians.

A: Anne

1. Be available to your shareholder/physician and protect their investment.

2. Be approachable for your managers, stay calm and pause to think in a crisis.

3. Be vigilant in monitoring key performance indicators.

Q: How do you balance your life and work?

A: Cinderella

My husband really helps me maintain that balance along with a great network of friends from both my personal and my business life.

A: LeeAnne

Being aware of the warning signs whether it be physical or mental. I also realize that there is no finish line and there will always be more work than I can handle at any given time.

A: Linda

We all have to draw our lines in a way we are most comfortable with. As I establish professional boundaries with staff and physicians, I carry that over into keeping personal life separate from business life. We have to demonstrate what we would like our employees to do. Balancing life and protecting personal time is one of those very important examples.

A: Anne

"Not terribly well."

She loves her job so much it is hard to let go of it sometimes.

(As I posed this question she immediately propelled into how much she loves her job!)

She will sometimes bring work home with her, but not necessarily to do it, but to maintain control if she feels like she really has to take care of it before the next day in the office. Anne also believes that while in the office, it is her time to create a presence and be there for the staff and physicians.

To make her personal time count the most, she is focused on times to spend with family that are true and treasured quality time. She also has a position that is much closer to her home.

Q: What are the best parts of healthcare that you would like to see carried forward?

A: LeeAnn

I would love to see the truly innovative solutions such as artificial intelligence (AI) and other integrative products continue to progress. I also like seeing disruptors that evolve and create a new way to do things.

I would like to carry forward the accessibility and increase the mutual responsibility and accountability that patients and physicians both have.

A: Linda

Technology is great but we cannot lose sight of keeping the patient front and center. That is most important.

Q: How do you establish a trusting rapport with physicians and staff?

A: LeeAnn

The most important factor to me is to learn who you are, what is most important for you as well as your perspective. Just as important is that we share with each other.

A: Cinderella

With physicians: You must walk the talk. I do not overshare.... Therefore they do not overshare with me. I am always professional with physicians—always. With staff:

- Being kind but strong at all times.
- Not being afraid to be seen as vulnerable in front of staff.
- Admit errors and move on.

A: Linda

Coming into this position I had been gradually moving up so the progression into this role was a smooth transition. With physicians: I start with listening: be present, be accessible and confidential. I never discuss one person with another.

I keep my personal details private and typically do not interact with anyone outside of work. When offering 'personal' information to anyone, such as what I did over the weekend, I offer that to everyone. To keep relationships 100 percent even, I'm not a friend to any staff or physician. (One can tell that Linda has the utmost integrity.)

A: June

With physicians: At one point I had to redefine the personal line and maintain professionalism with a physician. We established clear boundaries and built up trust over time.

With staff: Employee and job descriptions often help determine lines and boundaries with each staff member as well. I have observed that people testing the boundaries is ongoing, and needs to be outlined and addressed periodically.

It's all about communication and putting the owner's perspective into action. I need to be able to stay positive and avoid the drama zone. I have found that every problem when it's broken down usually results from a lack of communication.

A: Anne

Be honest.

Learn what is personally important to them.

Find out why they came to work or picked the practice and why they stay. I like to see how each employee says the practice and what their priorities are.

Anne also did not find any real challenges as the first female CEO of this group. The trust evolved in a positive natural evolution.

With establishing boundaries, she rarely socializes with co-workers unless it is a company function. It is most important to have colleagues and great friends outside of work who may work in different industries. This help separates the line between work and personal as well.

Q: How do you keep in touch with every staff member?

A: LeeAnn

I make it a point to do rounds each day. I may not make it to every floor and every department. Even a daily quick reach out, so I am visible every day.

A: Linda

My goal is to be at every location (4) every week. I get to know each person and call them by name. If I don't recall the staff person's name, I ask again. When I'm leaving any office I check in with each person to say "I'm headed to office xyz, do you need anything?" I want to convey that I am there for them … "What can I do for you?"

A: Anne

Anne sees staff members throughout the week while in the practice as everyone carries out their role or in the kitchen or lunchroom. This grants a casual conversation and a continued familiarity. She also attends every practice event.

Q: What are key factors that you take into consideration that balance your decision-making?

A: Cinderella

- How/Will this affect patient care?
- How/Will this affect my staff?
- How will this affect my P&L?

A: Linda

I always try to look at the big picture. When making a financial decision, how does that break down by number of providers, over how much time? I want to start with data and objective information on any decision, then move to subjective, if needed. It is also easier for them to accept when it is broken down and not one lump sum. The physician sees how it relates directly to them.

(Linda may at times move to subjective review after looking at issues objectively to ensure that the decision is also meeting practice goals.)

A: Anne

The first factor is that the physicians on the practice. It is my role to carry out their decisions on their behalf. Even if we may discuss behind closed doors, we stand united with the practice and its goals.

She is honest and truthful and considers how decisions may impact of the least interested, so she is sure to protect the interests evenly amongst shareholders.

Q: Is there an example of a time you had to defend a decision to the physicians and/or board?

A: Cinderella

Yes. There was a sharp increase in group health premiums. I refused to lower coverage or increase employee reimbursement levels. My board ultimately supported my decision. (She was able to emphasize the importance of the employees).

A: Anne

When defending a decision, Anne prefers to introduce an idea and let it sit a while for people to consider with a timing that is most comfortable for them.

Q: What are the most important characteristics of an executive /leader?

A: Cinderella

- Professionalism
- Kindness
- Ability to listen
- Ability to make thoughtful decisions

A: June

- ◆ Listening
- ◆ Provide perspective
- ◆ Create enthusiasm

13

Questions for
Peer Discussions

As we continually learn and advance, these questions can be useful for engaging conversations and posed at peer roundtable discussions. Remember, this is a great time to tap into others' knowledge and are perfect settings where we can glean a few beautiful "pearls!"

Ground Rules

- What is said here, stays here, pinky swear.
- Be honest. It's okay and, in fact, essential to get the most from these questions. This is the purpose of our discussions.
- Look for those ideas and the "between the lines" confirmations that help you ascertain the best of proven techniques for your practice.
- Unless you want a specific set up or structure, let the topics take you where you want to go. It's all about what your priorities are and what you would like to talk about. We tend to take a natural flow towards most prominent issues and what we need to discuss the most!
- Everyone has a voice and a story to tell. Give each person a chance to tell theirs.

When Your Daughter Buys You An "Anti-Stress Kit" For the Holidays

- How much do you love your role right now? Really?
- What are some methods or actions that help you mentally detach from work and really relax?
- What is your energy level like these days?
- Are you working too much? What would your best friend say?
- How often - and how much work are you doing on your own personal time at home?
- What are two things you would change about your position that could immediately lessen your daily stress level?
- Have you used all of your PTO/Leave time this year?
- Are you finding enough time for personal activities and hobbies?

Returning to Why We Are Here and Listening for What is Next

- What is your favorite story regarding a positive, thought-provoking or ethical situation that involved either individual staff members or practice wide?
- What three pieces of advice would you offer to a new medical manager?
- What characteristics and standard practices of traditional care are most important to you to conserve and remain a part of patient care?

- What factors about healthcare today make you excited about healthcare in the future?

- What do you need to continually improve?

- What is something that may be a moving target, or you just can't seem to get right? …And why do you think that is? (I know, many choices. Which are the most common in your group?)

Emotional Intelligence Essentials Questions

- Do you believe that you can be adequately aware of and control your emotions during an uncomfortable situation such as a confrontation with an angry staff member?

- Can you tell when another person is uncomfortable because of something you have said or done, even if unintentionally?

- Being aware of our "cues" is half the battle. What are some words, actions, kinds of people, emotions or events that "press your buttons"?

- Have you had any training in emotional intelligence? Such as onboarding? If so please share your experience.

- Are you able to remain calm and focused and a very emotional and stressful situation, such as dealing with an angry patient, employee, or physician?

- Please share a time when you have had to use your emotional intelligence in a very challenging situation.

- Can you walk into a room and sense that something has just gone on that you wish you were more aware of?

Hire First Class Staff—
And Hold On!

- What are your best resources and most successful venues for advertising administrative and nursing/clinical openings?

- What is your best pointer for retaining stellar employees?

- How are *you* recognized and/or rewarded?

- Do you have an annual staff meeting/picnic/corporate staff retreat?

- What step and/or strategy in your hiring process helps you reach a true *first* impression of the candidate?

- Do you conduct exit interviews? With every employee?

- What is your best story of when staff members supported each other? For example, covering holiday vacation time for an employee with extenuating circumstances.

- Do you perform skills, personality, or profile testing?

- In your personnel manual (beyond **HIPAA**, theft, harassment, etc.), what are some actions or events that can result in instant termination?

- Cite examples of how you display and relay a staff member's value within your practice?

- What are the top three reasons that a candidate would select to work for your practice or facility versus another?

- Do you have a performance improvement program in place? Does it work?

- What types of training are offered to staff members?

- Are your continuing education credit allowances a good/fair and competitive amount?

- Do you have a staff wellness program?

Emotional Intelligence— Financial and Revenue Cycle Management

- What kind of collections incentives, if any, do you offer your staff?
- What are some examples of recent and successful accounts receivable policies in your office?
- Do you conduct formal training for front desk time of service collections?
- What venues and platforms do you utilize to reach out specifically to high deductible and direct pay patients: online or other communications?
- At what point (or aging) do you typically turn patients over to an outside collection agency?
- Do you have staff perform internal collections before turning over to an outside entity?
- How do you know your billing staff is working to their full potential?
- Does your front desk believe that the billing department fully supports your front desk when needed?
- Do you have trainings to promote cultural understanding—such as emotional intelligence?
- Is your front desk trained on collecting from high deductible patients?

Build A Culture of Superior Communication

- How often do you have general staff meetings? Other, one on ones, departmental, and manager meetings?
- What is a recent action that you have taken to improve communication with your staff?

- Please think of an example of an extremely difficult experience with a miscommunication. How was is resolved?

- What is a recent action that you have taken to improve communication with your patients?

- Which department (and why) is the easiest to communicate with? And why?

- What is an example of an innovative tool that you have used for communication?

Time Management, Operations, and How to Protect Your Calendar

- How do you keep in touch and remain present in each staff member's workday?

- How often do you meet with managers (as a group and individually)?

- How much time do you typically allow for periodic one-on-one meetings?

- What is the most impactful thing you do to protect you time/calendar?

- Who most typically assigns staff members and creates committees for projects such as a new PM/EMR, ancillary service, etc.?

- How comfortable are you with delegating? Is it difficult for you? And why?

- Is there a balanced departmental representation when researching and exploring vendors, products and services?

- Beyond system updates, what kind of education does your staff receive to improve their performance?

- Are your employees aware their actions are tracked and reviewed?

Nuances that Can Affect Credibility

- How often do you set goals? Or do you just see where life takes you? There is no wrong answer, this is a matter of approach.

- Is there an example of an action, change, or unexpected event that ended up adding to your credibility in your staff member's view?

- Do you have a mentor?

- Have you or are you now mentoring?

- Can you give an example of where you have broken new ground within a limited culture?

- What person, factors, episode, or decision-making process helped you to become a healthcare professional vs. another industry?

- If you are a part of or have had experience with a family member as manager, please share as to the differences versus non-family members administrating a practice.

- If you are a new manager, what are your top concerns regarding your credibility within the practice?

- What actions do you take to aid in staff member's understanding of their co-workers' roles? The higher the turnover, the lower the percentage of understanding is due to the natural occurrence of cross training over a longer period of time.

- What nuances do you own that you think may work towards gaining staff trust and viewing you as a true leader?

The Provider's Role and Relationships—Trust and Support, Conflict and Resolutions

- How were you able to gain physicians' trust?

- How much do you believe that your and the physicians' goals are aligned?

- How often do you and providers meet regarding overall practice operations and financials?

Questions for Administrators/ Executives/Physicians

- What are three pieces of advice you would offer a new leader?

- What are key factors that you take into consideration that balance your decision-making?

- How did you establish a trusting rapport with the physicians and staff?

- How do you keep in touch with every staff member?

- Did you rise to your position within your practice or were you recruited from another? And did your specific circumstance make a difference in the staff's acceptance of your new role?

- How do you establish professional and personal boundaries with managers and physicians?

- As a new CEO/Leader/Physician, what are the first five things you would do upon entering the practice?

- Is there an example of a time you had to defend a decision to the physicians and/or board?

- What are the most essential characteristics of a successful physician/executive /leader?

- What are the best things about traditional and conventional healthcare that you perceive most important and carry forward?

- What are the most challenging issues in healthcare you would like to see changed, and how would you change them?

- What would you tell someone today that is interested in starting their own practice?

- Beyond the healing, what is the most important things we can do for a patient?

Author Biography

Susan Fink Childs, FACMPE

The founder of Evolution Healthcare Consulting, Susan Childs has over thirty years' experience in healthcare and is a Board-Certified Fellow of the American College of Medical Practice Executives (ACMPE). Her recognized professionalism and trusted and proven approaches help practices establish conscious processes and strategies that encourage and promote self-awareness, creating high performance teams.

Susan has an extensive background in medical practice operations, personnel, revenue cycle, front desk collections, communication, customer service, and physician communications. She uses this experience to guide dynamic and fruitful staff workshops and practice retreats.

She is a national presenter for many organizations, including AAP, AAOE, MGMA, ASCENT, ACC, and the AMA. Susan also served as the ACMPE Advancement Chair with MGMA.

Ms. Child's objective is to help practices build compassionate, accessible care, while also ensuring they recognize the positive impact and value of each staff member.

Endnotes and Resources

1   *CNBC.com*, https://www.cnbc.com/2019/04/01/85percent-of-us-workers-are-happy-with-their-jobs-national-survey-shows.html, David Spiegel April 2019

2   *Huffington Post*, Brittany Wong, 07/25/2019, Updated July 26, 2019 https://www.huffpost.com/entry/niksen-dutch-word-for-doing-nothing_l_5d-37852be4b004b6adb788ff ; Time, Sophia Gottfried, 07/12/2019, https://time.com/5622094/what-is-niksen/)

3   https://www.sleepfoundation.org/articles/how-much-sleep-do-we-really-need

4   https://www.nih.gov/news-events/news-releases/brain-may-flush-out-toxins-during-sleep, October 17, 2013

5   *Foods That Help Battle Depression*, Elizabeth Bernstein April 2, 2018

6   From *Everything In Its Place: First Loves and Last Tales*, Oliver Sacks, republished May 2019

7   The Importance Of Emotional Intelligence In The Work Place: Why It Matters More Than Personality, Mike Posekey, Zerorisk GHR, Inc, 2019

8   MGMA STAT April 2019

9   HR Dive Brief August 2017, Valerie Bolden-Barrett https://www.hrdive.com/news/study-turnover-costs-employers-15000-per-worker/449142/

10 https://www.dailypay.com/blog/employee-turnover-rates-in-the-healthcare-industry/ November 2018

11 Transgender Law Center, Model Transgender Employment Policy, 2019

12 *FastCompany.com*, Harvey Deutschendorf, June 26, 2019 https://www.fastcompany.com/40588344/4-emotionally-intelligent-hr-policies-employees-may-suffer-without

13 https://www.entrepreneur.com/article/318187, Rose Leadem

14 *LinkedIn*, March 20, 2020, Lisa Bailey https://www.theconnectedproject.com lisa@theconnectedproject.com

15 Institute For Health And Human Potential, Can EQ make you more money than IQ?, Bill Benjamin, January 2017

16 Leaderships Freak Blog, October 3, 2019, the-10-laws-of-trust—the-chairman-of-jet-blue

17 https://www.talentsmart.com/about/emotional-intelligence.php, Travis Bradberry, 2019

18 https://www.talentsmart.com/articles/7-Things-Great-Listeners-Do-Differently-386889568-p-1.html Travis Bradberry, 2019

19 https://www.wsj.com/articles/use-mirroring-to-connect-with-others-1474394329 "Use Mirroring to Connect with Others", Sue Shellenbarger, Sept 20, 2016 (paywall)

20 "Use Mirroring to Connect with Others," Sue Shellenbarger, Sept 20, 2016

21 https://www.inc.com/geoffrey-james/adios-powerpoint-this-simple-document-template-makes-meetings-shorter-sweeter-smarter.html

22 *MailOnline*, Daniel Bates, "People are distracted by their phone even when they *aren't* using it, study clamis," 12/9/2014

23 Institute For Health and Human Potential, 2009, https://www.ihhp.com/wp-content/uploads/whitepapers/roi_for_emotional_intelligen.pdf

24 https://www.healthleadersmedia.com/clinical-care/new-stanford-childrens-health-ceo-impacting-childs-life-intoxicating, Christopher Cheney, October 23, 2019

25 *Forbes.com*, New Science Shows It's Better To Praise People For Their Successes Than To Correct Their Mistakes, Mark Travers, MD, Nov 11, 2019 https://www.forbes.com/sites/traversmark/2019/11/11/new-science-shows-its-better-to-praise-people-for-their-successes-than-to-correct-their-failures/#4bcd091d2d87 original study: https://journals.sagepub.com/doi/full/10.1177/0956797619881133

26 *Inc.com*, T.H.I.N.K. Before You Speak, https://www.inc.com/lee-colan/think-before-you-speak.html, August 14, 2020

Resources

1. *Emotional Intelligence 2.0*, Travis Bradberry and Jean Greaves 2009

2. *How to Win Friends and Influence People*, Dale Carnegie

CPSIA information can be obtained
at www.ICGtesting.com
Printed in the USA
LVHW081058191021
700840LV00006B/91/J